D6 Family Ministry Journal

Published by Randall House Academic
www.randallhouse.com

Editors

Why the need for another journal?

Over the last decade, the Deuteronomy 6 (D6) scriptural principle has shifted ministry philosophy in two areas. The first area challenges ministry leaders to evaluate how to inspire and equip parents and grandparents to disciple at home and to champion Christ and Scripture in everyday life. The second area encourages preschool, children, student, and adult ministries to have healthy handoffs and collaboration from one age to the next.

As seminaries and universities change their teaching to incorporate both philosophy shifts, the need developed for a journal that supported the intentional home emphasis as part of ministry. The D6 Family Journal combines academic peer-reviewed articles along with a limited selection of practitioner insights and, of course, book reviews on recent family ministry titles.

Purpose Statement

The purpose of D6 Family Ministry Journal is to support the thinking and practices of parenting in Christian homes, in family ministry in the local church, and in parachurch settings that reflect God's intent for generational discipleship as presented in Deuteronomy 6 and other biblical texts. This purpose is achieved by the publication of articles and essays that do the following:

- Reflect on the scriptural foundations of God's use of paternal and maternal influences in the lives of children and grandchildren while also acknowledging various contemporary family situations
- Explore the integration and application of the relationship between the church and home
- Support the teaching of generational approaches to Christian education at colleges and seminaries for the equipping of ministry leaders and parents
- Champion methodologies that prepare children and young adults in the development of a Christian lifestyle and Christian leadership skills

The journal is primarily intended for two audiences: an academic community of professors and students in institutions of higher learning who are committed to the development of a new generation of Christian ministers and community leaders. Second, those professionals who are already serving in local church and parachurch settings. In order to facilitate discussion and learning among both groups, each publication will:

- Provide publishing opportunities primarily for:
  academic peer reviewed work
  practitioner insights

- Offer a platform for research into family ministry
- Review new books connected to generational discipleship and classic texts and family ministry related fields

Manuscripts for publication should be directed to the attention of the managing editor at the following address: 114 Bush Road, Nashville, TN, 37217. Email inquiries should be sent to academic@d6family.com.

© 2016 by Randall House Academic
Printed in the United States of America
ISBN 9780892659852

Contents

Editorial

Articles

Practitioner Insights

Book Reviews

Editorial

Families are a key component of God's work in the world. From the joining of Adam and Eve, the Mosaic commands of Deuteronomy 6, King David's dysfunctional family relationships, to the New Testament Household Codes, family life plays a defining part in the Bible's dramatic narrative. For those who may doubt the importance of family within God's unfolding story of redemption, recall that the focal point of Scripture, Jesus, does not appear fully grown from the heavens. He is born into a family that protects and nurtures Him until the fullness of time. With all of the attention given to families and the ordering of familial relationships in the Bible, it is no surprise that much thought focused on church renewal revolves around the special relationship between churches and families.

Into the current conversations that inform the present day church and family dynamic comes the Journal you are reading; the D6 Family Ministry Journal. This Journal aims to positively contribute to the broader Church and Home discussion through scholarly research focused on practical implications. It is the desire of the Journal's editorial board that the research and implications suggested in the D6 Family Ministry Journal reinforce thinking and practices that reflect God's intent for generational discipleship. In order to carry out this aim, each Journal edition will contain both academic, peer reviewed essays and practical insights by assorted teachers and practitioners of Church and Home ministry.

For those familiar with the D6 role within the Church and Home movement, this Journal appears as the logical next step in an undertaking spearheaded by Randall House since 2004. The D6 impact on the Church and Home movement is rooted in a commitment to the centrality of the classic imperatives of Deuteronomy 6:5-7. Recognizing the biblical directive for parents to teach and train children according to the Lord's Word is for all believers, Randall House, who holds trademark to D6, has spent considerable energy over the past 12 years facilitating countless conversations, overseeing family focused church curriculum, and hosting the annual D6 conference. These efforts are characterized by an intentional willingness to listen to Scripture and seasoned voices from diverse backgrounds and differing church traditions. This journal functions as yet another opportunity to bring minds and hearts together for collaboration around generational discipleship.

Building off their established track record, Randall House hopes that the D6 Journal will serve as a helpful tool in facilitating sound theory and practices. In line with Randall House's desire to hear from diverse participants in the Church and Home conversation, this first edition contains voices from Christian higher education, leaders within local churches, and practitioners from para-church organizations. Authors include both men and women, those who minister in higher profile ministries and those who labor in less known locales. Some articles are research heavy, while others are more focused on exposition of biblical passages informing Church and Home discussions. However, each author's personal story and each article's focus notwithstanding, readers will find that every article contains appropriate argumentation, clarity, and a commitment to both the Church and Home. If readers find within these pages' discussion that encourages biblical fidelity, challenges creative thinking, and at times ignites reasoned disagreement, then this Journal will have made the contribution desired by Randall House to furthering the Church and Home movement.

Charles Cook
Managing Editor, D6 Family Ministry Journal

Equipping Youth in the Home to Face the Challenges of Today and Tomorrow

Edward E. Moody Jr.

Abstract: As young adults, many Christians have experienced difficulty applying their faith to everyday life. In this paper we examine dilemma discussions, a cognitive developmental technique that has been found to successfully impact behavior. A model is proposed whereby parents can utilize dilemma discussions to help their children effectively address problems they face in everyday life while preparing them to apply their faith to successfully navigate adulthood.

Keywords: dilemma discussions, applying faith to everyday life, D6

The difficulty that young Christian adults have experienced applying the Scripture to daily life has been well documented. Barna (2007) has noted that in several areas there were no statistical differences between the lives of people who described themselves as born-again Christians and those who did not. Christians were statistically as likely to gamble, visit pornographic websites, take something that did not belong to them, consult a psychic, physically fight or abuse someone, consume enough alcohol to get intoxicated, to have used an illegal drug, said something untrue, sought revenge, or talked badly about someone behind their back as non Christians. Young Christian adults have been described by many nonbelievers as out of touch and unable to effectively interact with people different from themselves leaving nonbelievers to perceive Christianity as anti-intellectual and stifling curiosity (Kinnaman & Lyons, 2007).

It appears that many young Christians have been ill-prepared to face a culture that overwhelms them and overly influences them. Perhaps there is a gap between instruction and the application of Scripture in our churches and homes. Christian adults, who grew up in Christian homes, may not have had periods where they grappled with how to apply the Bible to real life issues. If we conclude that Christian youth need help applying their faith to daily life, it would be wise to examine some approaches that have been used in other settings to help youth interact more effectively with others. Cognitive developmental techniques have been found to be effective helping youth to take on the perspectives of others and to improve their ability to interact well with other youth (Rest & Thoma, 1986). Perhaps we can utilize lessons from cognitive development theories that have been used to improve behavior in youth and stimulate their ability to deal with life issues.

Cognitive Development Theory

In this paper we will look at ways to adapt cognitive development techniques for use in the home to help prepare youth to deal with the challenges they face at school and in the community as well as to prepare them for the challenges they will encounter in the future. The aim of this paper is not to review cognitive developmental theories, but a brief background should be helpful to the reader.

After Piaget, the best-known cognitive developmental theorist is Lawrence Kohlberg, who developed a theory of moral development. Kohlberg's theory consists of three levels, each with two stages. Level one, the preconventional level, is characteristic of children ages 9 to 11. This level consists of two stages. Stage one involves an obedience and punishment orientation. An individual decides what is right to do based on fear of punishment. Stage two involves satisfying ones needs and only occasionally satisfying the needs of others. Level two, the conventional level, involves Stage three reasoning where right action is characterized by receiving approval from one's peers, and to be pleasing to others. This person responds to praise and wants others to like them. Stage four is often called the law and order stage that is characterized by an orientation to doing one's duty and showing respect for authority. The postconventional level consists of two stages where customs and social rules are examined in terms of universal moral principles. At stage five, the individual is concerned with doing the greatest good for the greatest number of people. Stage six was the highest point on the Kohlberg's development ladder and involved the moral point of view in its purest form, even if one's decision might bring harm to themselves (Jennings, Kilkenny, & Kohlberg, 1983; Sprinthall, 1978).

Dilemma Discussions

Kohlberg and his colleagues hypothesized that as people develop, the manner in which they perceive relationships and their responsibilities to others changes from an egocentric to other-perspective resulting in upward movement through his proposed stages (Rest, Cooper, Coder, Masanz, & Anderson, 1974). To help people move from an egocentric worldview to other-perspective, Kohlberg and his colleagues developed dilemma discussion groups (Kohlberg & Mayer, 1972). In this approach, youth are presented with a dilemma and asked, "What is the right thing to do in this situation?" As the youth discusses the dilemma under the guidance of a counselor, they are exposed to the perspectives of other members in their group. They also learn that it is difficult to resolve issues when one utilizes only egocentric approaches.

When dilemma discussions are discussed over a significant period of time (usually the equivalent of one academic semester), they have proven to be effective in stimulating perspective taking, indicating this is not simply an intellectual exercise (Rest & Thoma, 1986). In fact, dilemma discussion groups have been used with success to help youth who struggle with their behavior, including violent and delinquent youth (Claypoole, Moody, & Peace, 2000; Gibbs, Potter, Goldstein, & Brendtro, 1996; Leeman, Gibbs, & Fuller, 1993). In Kohlberg's approach, the focus is upon what is the right thing to do. The way a person thinks about an issue appears to impact how they behave. Perhaps taking the time to analyze and think about how one will address an issue helps the youth to deal with everyday problems.

Selman's Interpersonal Negotiation Strategies

Another cognitive development theorist, Robert Selman, developed a theory focused upon interpersonal negotiation strategies. He too utilized dilemma discussions, however, his approach appears to be more application oriented with four functional steps. Step one is to define the problem. After a youth is presented with a dilemma they are asked, "What is the problem?" as they clarify what the issue is they are better equipped to address it. Step two is to generate alternative strategies. The goal is to think of more than one way to solve the problem at hand. Step three is selecting and implementing a specific strategy. In this step, the youth is helped to examine the consequences of a particular action. After an approach is chosen, one might work with the youth and even role-play attempting to implement a solution. Step four is to evaluate the outcome. How did it go? As a young person becomes able to evaluate outcomes, they increase their level of problem solving sophistication (Schultz, Yeates, & Selman, 1989). This type of dilemma discussion intervention has been used with pairs of incarcerated youth and found to be effective in improving their behavior (Moody, 1999). With Selman's approach, the focus is upon what to do and how to handle a particular problem.

Could Parents Use Dilemma Discussions?

Since dilemma discussions take place in groups, it initially appears that they could not be used in a home environment. Indeed, most of the research on dilemma discussions has taken place in group settings like prisons, schools, and colleges (Rest & Thoma, 1986). However, there was a classic study conducted by Walker and Taylor (1991) that indicated that dilemma discussions conducted by parents could be effective.

Walker and Taylor (1991) perceived that cognitive development theorists like Piaget and Kohlberg were biased against parents, perhaps reacting against Freud's psychoanalytic theory where parents seemed to be responsible for all of the hardships their child might experience in adulthood. They considered this bias to be unfounded. They implemented an intervention whereby a father, mother, and child engaged in dilemma discussions using hypothetical and real life dilemmas over a two year period. Their results indicated that children whose parents discussed the dilemmas with them utilizing Socratic questioning (open ended, probing questions), supportive interactions (encouraging them to say what they thought), along with higher level reasoning, experienced growth (Walker & Taylor, 1991). Could this be a model Christian parents could utilize?

Christianity and Cognitive Development Theory

Before proceeding, we might ask, "Are cognitive developmental approaches appropriate for use by Christians?" Some Christian psychologists have suggested that Kohlberg's theory is compatible with a Christian worldview and pointed out that there are corollaries with Christian teachings that urge the Christian to move beyond both self-centered morality and a morality founded in human traditions (Clouse, 1985; Joy, 1983a; McNeel, 1991; Motet, 1978; Ward, 1979). Gibson (2004) critiqued Kohlberg's theory and utilized insights from it when he proposed four levels of spiritual maturity: accommodation to God's law, respect for and obedience to God's law, principle-centered commitment to a Christian worldview, and kingdom-centered commitment to God's glory.

However, in many ways cognitive developmental theories fall short. Joy (1983b) criticized Kohlberg in particular for not acknowledging the human capacity for going astray at every stage of life. Balswick, King, and Reimer (2005) noted that Kohlberg failed to account for the theological motivations that guide a person's actions in life, and Moroney (2006) questioned using Kohlberg's framework of lower and higher stages of moral reasoning prescriptively.

Clearly there are pros and cons to cognitive developmental theories. In the remainder of this paper, we will look at using dilemma discussions with a biblical focus. Though we will be utilizing cognitive developmental techniques, cognitive developmental theorists would quickly point out that what follows is not a cognitive developmental approach. Indeed, we might say what follows is a biblical approach that borrows some cognitive developmental techniques to help youth apply their faith to everyday life, while preparing them for the future.

Conducting Dilemma Discussions at Home

Dilemma discussions did not begin with cognitive developmental theorists, as any reader of the Bible knows. Dilemmas and parables are seen throughout the Scripture with Nathan's story about a lamb told to David to confront him about his actions with Bathsheba, to Jesus' use of the

Good Samaritan story to teach us about how to love our neighbors. In Deuteronomy 6:7, parents are instructed to diligently teach their children in the home, when they walk (or drive) along the way, when they lie down, and when they rise. Certainly this admonition includes teaching how to apply Scripture.

Family Sessions

Walker and Taylor (1991) used dilemmas in what they referred to as "family sessions," which lasted for 20 to 60 minutes. The length of each discussion can vary. It is the frequency rather than the length that matters (Moody & Lupton-Smith, 1999). We suggest a similar time frame where the family begins the process by discussing dilemmas from the Bible. For example, a parent might read Esther 4:1-11 and ask, "What should Esther do?" Examples of other biblical dilemmas that could be utilized are found in Table 1.

Later, parents can begin presenting hypothetical dilemmas and ask their child, "What is the right thing to do?" about each issue. After some discussion ensues a parent can ask, "What does the Bible say about this issue?" The goal is to get the child in the habit of looking toward the Bible whenever a dilemma or problem arises. For example, a parent might present the problem Daniel faced about eating the king's food (Daniel 1:5-7). After a discussion about whether it would be right to eat the food, the parent might ask "What does the Scripture say?" and point out that Leviticus 11 forbade eating the food that was likely offered to Daniel. A parent might then ask a child to consider which issues they might face that are similar to the one faced by Daniel.

There is great value to thinking about Scripture. Ariely (2012) asked college students in his class to recall the Ten Commandments. Though none of his students could recall all of the Ten Commandments, and many described themselves as nonreligious, they were significantly less likely to cheat after thinking about the Ten Commandments. It is always good when a young person is spending some time thinking about Scripture.

Perspective Taking

In each dilemma, the youth should be asked to consider the issue from the standpoint of the various characters in the story (e., g., Esther, Mordecai, Haman, Ahasuerus). One of the goals of dilemma discussions is to help someone take on the perspective of another person as Nathan used the parable about how the only lamb of a man was taken away from him. David examined the event from the perspective of the man whose lamb head been taken, which enabled David to comprehend the full weight of his own actions in the taking of Bathsheba. The Scripture teaches us to take the perspective of others. Paul wrote to look to the interests of others (Philippians 2:4), and Jesus instructed us to do unto others as we would want them to do to us (Luke 6:31).

How does this work in a dilemma discussion? In a discussion about the parable of the Good Samaritan a parent might begin by asking, "What is the right thing to do?" regarding helping the wounded man. As the discussion continues, they can ask, "How do you think the wounded man felt?" "How do you think the Levite felt?" "How do you think the priest felt?" and so forth. This helps the child view an issue from multiple perspectives. As a child begins to examine multiple perspectives it helps them understand and relate better to other people. Paul described perspective taking to us in 1 Corinthians 9:19-23 as he described identifying with the Jews, those under the law, those outside the law, and the weak, to reach them.

To teach this technique a parent might use the situation found in Daniel 1 where Daniel was told to eat forbidden food when he was a slave in Babylon. As one defines the problem they might ask, "Why would Nebuchadnezzar require the food to be eaten?" Regarding the eunuch, "Why would he want the food to be eaten?" For Daniel, "Why doesn't Daniel want to eat this food?" The goal is for the child to see each person's perspective. Nebuchadnezzar likely required the food to be eaten because he was pursuing a particular regimen to be followed so as to ensure success. The eunuch likely wanted Daniel and his friends to succeed. Perhaps he would have been promoted if they achieved, it appears likely he would have been in grave danger had Daniel and his friends failed (Daniel 1:10). Interestingly, as you look at the story you can see that Daniel took on the perspective of the eunuch, the steward, and Nebuchadnezzar as he addressed this problem (Daniel 1:12-13).

Nonthreatening Environment

These discussions can be challenging to a parent as they may be disappointed by some of the thoughts and beliefs they hear. Often as youth are asked to discuss the Good Samaritan they begin to discuss issues of class and prejudice as well as motivation derived from fear and self-interest. For dilemma discussions to work, there needs to be a nonthreatening environment where interaction flows freely (Gomberg, Cameron, Fenton, Purtek, & Hill, 1980; Kuhmerker, 1991). This can be difficult for parents as the authority in the home. Parents who are willing to let their children grapple with a problem without immediately prescribing a solution will find that real developmental growth takes place over time (Walker & Taylor, 1991). Consider the situation Jonathan and David faced recorded in 1 Samuel 18-20. One can discuss with their child what is the right thing for Jonathan to do with regard to telling his father Saul about the location of David. After examining the dilemma from the perspective of Jonathan, David, and Saul, a parent might develop another dilemma about whether they would help a classmate who rivaled them for the highest grade in the class or a peer who competed with them for a starting position on the team or a co-worker who might excel to the point of receiving a promotion that one was in line to receive. If children are honest, they (and often we) struggle to behave as Jonathan believed. Jonathan's actions reveal that he was a man skillful at applying the Scripture and doing what was right even when it was very hard to do. Continued discussion and examination of the Scripture will lead to growth. The right answer today, is not as important as being able to behave rightly tomorrow.

Problem Solving

In addition to looking at what is the right thing to do, dilemmas can be used to teach problem-solving skills. This approach is borrowed from Robert Selman's Interpersonal Negotiation Strategies. We have already discussed perspective taking which is very valuable as a youth attempts to resolve an issue with another person. In a problem-solving dilemma, the first goal is to define the problem.

After a discussion about what is the right thing for Daniel to do, one might examine the dilemma from a problem-solving perspective. Some will define the problem as something like "I'm being told to do something that the Scripture teaches as wrong." In our dilemma discussions we add a step to the problem-solving approach, which is "What does the Bible say about this issue? In looking at the issue we may find that the Bible forbids us to do what we are being told to do (as was the case with Daniel). We may also find guidance in the Scripture for how to deal with the issue. Though Daniel did not have access to Matthew 18, he utilized this principle when he likely privately discussed this issue first with the eunuch.

Step two is to generate alternatives. Daniel likely used two alternatives that he generated. First, he went to the chief of the eunuchs (Daniel 1:10), when that did not work he went to the steward (Daniel 1:11). After he spoke to the chief of the eunuchs he evaluated the outcome and tried another alternative. Parents can work with their children to help them generate solutions to problems and select an appropriate strategy to implement. This process reminds us of Jesus' admonition to "first sit down and count the cost" as we follow Him (Luke 14:26-30).

Step three is to implement a strategy. Daniel did this by requesting that the chief of the eunuchs not force him to eat the food (Daniel 1:8-10). Though the eunuch empathized with Daniel, he did not grant Daniel's request. Daniel appears to have quickly engaged in step four that involves evaluating the outcome as he then approached the steward with a request and a solution (Daniel 1:11-16). Daniel's perspective taking skill allowed him to work effectively with the steward and achieve his objective. Similarly, a parent might discuss a plan A and B strategy with their child. They may even be able to help them with step four as they evaluate outcomes to this first attempt. A child who regularly engages in this process will learn how to naturally solve various life issues.

Guiding Discussions

Good questioning, reflecting, and probing skills are essential to conducting successful dilemma discussions. Questions and probes should be used to keep the discussion going, to challenge thinking, and encourage a youth to take multiple perspectives. Open-ended questions like "What should he do?" and "What do you think?" keep the child thinking and working. Frequently reflecting the child's responses with statements like, "So you think he should try to help the man" guide the discussion. The goal is to help the child clarify their position and to take the steps needed to address the problem. A good rule to follow is for each question the parent asks they provide at least one paraphrase of the response. Closed questions that can be answered with a yes or no response can be used when trying to move to a different subject. At the end of each discussion a summary statement about what has transpired helps the youth tie everything together.

When presenting a dilemma ask the child to read it and get their initial reaction. Sometimes it helps to write down initial reactions on a dry erase board. If you have more than one child and there are differences, a debate can be set up. Help them see problems with their reasoning by examining consequences of particular actions.

Every perspective of the consequence of each action does not have to be discussed. Ideally a discussion is ended while the youth is still interested. That creates the possibility that they will discuss and think about the dilemma later. Keep the discussion moving and try to be spontaneous. Keep it interesting and fun. When the discussion seems to lag, role-play the action in the dilemma and some of their proposals for dealing with it. Spice up the discussion by using role-play, videos, movies, current events, and field trips that complement the dilemmas.

Parents can use their creativity in the creation of dilemmas. In Appendix A, there is a dilemma called the "Cheat Sheet." The dilemma is straightforward about whether one should cheat and easily leads itself to a discussion about what is the right thing to do and what does the Scripture say about the issue? After a discussion about this dilemma, a parent can utilize "I Missed That Class," which deals with whether one should tell on a peer who cheats. Finally, "I Can't Get Up" brings home the consequences of cheating. Parents can design dilemmas that help their children address important issues from different perspectives.

Real Life Dilemmas

It is important that real-life dilemmas be utilized that the youth can see themselves encountering (Locke, 1983). Use dilemmas that arise at school, in the community, and from current events. Youth can also be given assignments to bring in their own dilemmas for discussion that can provide rich information about the struggles they face.

Walker and Taylor (1991) found the real life dilemmas that youth discussed with their parents led to the greatest growth. Often a parent and child, in the refuge of their home, are able to define the problem and generate alternatives easily. As they select a strategy they are able to take their time and look at what the Bible says about the particular issue. The parent and child may role-play implementing the strategy in the home and even talk it through again before implementing it. After the child implements the strategy, they can process how it went with the parent and make adjustments where needed. As they utilize the Bible in this process they are living Deuteronomy 6. As the child learns how to apply the Bible to daily problems they are gaining skills that will help them throughout their lives.

Summary

It appears that dilemma discussions could be used in the home to teach youth how to apply Scripture to the problems they encounter in life, thereby preparing them to face more complicated problems in the future. Though dilemma discussions are derived from cognitive developmental techniques, similar formats appear to have been utilized by Jesus and past prophets. We recommend preparing families to utilize these tools so their children may be better equipped to face the challenges of life.

References

Ariely, D. (2012). *The (honest) truth about dishonesty.* New York, NY: Harper Collins.

Barna Group (2007). 4 American Lifestyles Mix Compassion and Self-Oriented Behavior. Assessed at https://www.barna.org/barna-update/donors-cause/110-american-lifestyles-mix-compassion-and-self-oriented-behavior#.Ve3JOrRTUdc on September 1, 2015.

Balswick, J. O., King, P. E., & Reimer, K. S. (2005). *The reciprocating self: Human development in theological perspective.* Downer's Grove, IL: InterVarsity Press.

Claypoole, S. D., Moody, E. E., & Peace, S. D. (2000). Moral dilemma discussions: An effective group intervention for juvenile offenders. *Journal for Specialists in Group Work, 25*(4), 349-411.

Clouse, B. (1985). *Moral development: Perspectives in psychology and Christian belief.* Grand Rapids, MI: Baker.

Gibbs, J. C., Potter, G. B., Goldstein, A. P. & Brendtro, L. K. (1996). Frontiers in psychoeducation: The EQUIP model with antisocial youth. *Reclaiming Children and Youth,* Winter, 22-28.

Gibson, T. S. (2004). Proposed levels of Christian spiritual maturity. *Journal of Psychology and Theology, 32,* 295-304.

Gomberg, S. H., Cameron, D. K., Fenton, E., Purtek, J. & Hill, C. L. (1980). *Leading dilemma discussions: A workshop.* Pittsburgh, PA: Carnegie Mellon University.

Jennings, W. S., Kilkenny, R., & Kohlberg, L. (1983). Moral development theory and practice for youthful and adult offenders. In W. S. Laufer & J. M. Day (Eds.). *Personality theory, moral development, and criminal behavior* (pp. 281-355). Toronto, Canada: Lexington Books.

Joy, D. M. (1983a). Introduction: Life is pilgrimage: In D. M. Joy (Ed., *Moral Development Foundations: Judeo-Christian alternatives to Piaget/Kohlberg.* Nashville, TN: Abingdon Press.

Joy, D. M. (1983b). Kohlberg revisited: A supra-naturalist speaks his mind: In D. M. Joy (Ed., *Moral Development Foundations: Judeo-Christian alternatives to Piaget/Kohlberg.* Nashville, TN: Abingdon Press.

Kinnaman, D., & Lyons, G. (2007). *Unchristian: What a new generation really thinks about Christianity . . . and why it matters.* Grand Rapids, MI: Baker Books.

Kohlberg, L., & Mayer, R. (1972). Development as the aim of education. *Harvard Educational Review, 42,* 449-496.

Kuhmerker, L. (1991). From theory to practice: Kohlberg's participation in secondary school programs. In L. Kuhmerker (Ed.), *The Kohlberg legacy for the helping professions.* Birmingham, AL: R.E.P. Books.

Leeman, L. W., Gibbs, J. C., & Fuller, D. (1993). Evaluation of a multi-component treatment program for juvenile delinquents. *Aggressive Behavior, 19,* 281-292.

Locke, D. (1983). Doing what comes morally: The relation between behavior and stage of moral reasoning. *Human Development, 26*, 11-25.

McNeel, S. P. (1991). Christian liberal arts education and growth in moral judgment. *Journal of Psychology and Christianity, 10*, 311-322.

Moody, E. E. (1999). Using pair counseling to reduce violence in youth offenders. In A. Reiman (Chair), *Social role taking and guided reflection: Deliberate interventions to promote ethical, intellectual, and interpersonal development.* Symposium conducted at the meeting of the Association for Moral Education, The University of Minnesota, Minneapolis, MN.

Moody, E. E., & Lupton-Smith, H. S. (1999). Interventions with juvenile offenders: Strategies to prevent acting out behavior. *Journal of Addictions & Offender Counseling, 20*, 2-14.

Moroney, S. K. (2006). Higher stages? Some cautions for Christian integration with Kohlberg's theory. *Journal of Psychology and Theology, 34*(4), 361-371.

Motet, D. (1978). Kohlberg's theory of moral development and the Christian faith. *Journal of Psychology and Theology, 6*, 18-21.

Rest, J., & Thoma, S. J. (1986). Educational programs and interventions. In J. R. Rest (Ed.) *Moral development: Advances in research and theory* (pp. 59-88). New York, NY: Praeger Publishers.

Rest, J., Cooper, D., Coder, R., Masanz, J., & Anderson, D. (1974). Judging the important issues in moral dilemmas: An objective measure of development. *Developmental Psychology, 10*, 491-501.

Schultz, L. H., Yeates, K. O., & Selman, R. L. (1989). *Interpersonal Negotiation Strategies Interview Manual.* Cambridge, MA: Harvard University.

Sprinthall, J. (1978). A primer on development. In N. Sprinthall & R. Mosher (Eds.), *Value development as the aim of education* (pp.1-15). Schenectady, NY: Character Education Press.

Walker, L. J., & Taylor, J. H. (1991). Family interactions and the development of moral reasoning. *Child Development, 62*(1), 264-283.

Ward, T. (1979). *Values begin at home.* Wheaton, IL: Victor Books.

Author Biography

Edward E. Moody Jr. is Chair of the Department of Allied Professions, and Professor of Counselor Education at North Carolina Central University in Durham, North Carolina and Pastor of Tippett's Chapel Free Will Baptist Church in Clayton, North Carolina.

Correspondence regarding this article may be sent to emoody@nccu.edu or Dr. Edward E. Moody Jr., North Carolina Central University, Department of Allied Professions, School of Education, 700 Cecil Street, Durham, North Carolina, 27707.

Table 1

Examples of Dilemmas Found in Scripture

Dilemma	Passage	Key Character(s)
Should Abraham Rescue Lot	Genesis 14	Abraham, Lot
Should She Stay or Should She Go?	Genesis 24	Abraham's servant, Isaac, Rebekah, Abraham, Laban
What Should Joseph Do?	Genesis 39	Joseph, Potiphar, Potiphar's wife
What Should Joseph do with his Brothers?	Genesis 42-45	Joseph, Joseph's brothers
Is It Worth It? The Midwives Risk Their Lives	Exodus 1	Midwives, Pharaoh
Oops! We Made the Wrong Deal	Joshua 9	Joshua, Elders
Leave or Cleave	Ruth 1	Ruth, Naomi, Orpah
Should You Try to Save a Bad Man?	1 Samuel 25	Abigail, Nabal, David
What Should She Do?	Esther 4	Esther, Mordcai, Haman
Can the Prodigal Son Come Home?	Luke 15	Father, older brother
Would You Help Saul/Paul?	Acts 9, 11	Ananias, Barnabas

Should John Mark Get	
a Second Chance?	Acts 15:36-40 Paul, Barnabas, John
	Mark, Silas

Appendix A

Cheat Sheet

Victoria has a friend who has obtained the answers to her final biology exam. Victoria has been struggling to make good grades because the top students in her graduating class are eligible for scholarships to colleges. She has been working hard and needs the money. She also knows that only the students with the best grades are recruited to the top colleges. Lately she has not had a lot of time to study because she has been working. To complicate matters many say the tests her teacher gives are brutal and have little to do with what is covered in class or the textbook. Everyone else will probably cheat so why shouldn't she?

I Missed That Class

Marcus is a third year medical resident at Mercy University Hospital. He is doing pretty well, but one of the surgical residents, Dr. Victoria Johnson, is struggling. It is as if she never went to medical school. A couple of times Marcus has stopped Victoria just before she did something bad. Yesterday she almost cut the main artery on a boy's leg because she did not know where to make the incision. She's going to kill someone if she gets to practice medicine on her own. People think she must have cheated to get where she is. Rumors abound that she began cheating way back in high school. Marcus doesn't want to cause any trouble but he doesn't want anyone to get hurt either. What should he do?

Questions to think about:

1. Do we have a responsibility to stop others from cheating?
2. What if Marcus confronts Victoria but she says she doesn't have a problem and that Marcus should mind his own business?

I Can't Get Up!

One day your little sister is doing gymnastics when she falls badly off the balance beam. At first she cries a lot and then yells, "I can't get up!" She can't move and the coaches believe she has injured her spine. She is rushed to the hospital where Dr. Victoria Johnson begins to work on her. Do you want her to operate on your sister?

Toward a Biblical Foundation for Curriculum

Amanda Cooley

Curriculum resource choices are critical for any and all educational settings, and especially the curriculum of the church, since it has eternal effects. Curriculum resources can affect the spiritual health and eternal destiny of individuals either negatively or positively. The value of children to God that is found in Scripture and the warnings not to cause children to stray from faith, intensify the need for curriculum evaluation.

Children in the Bible

From the very beginning, God included children in His creation. Genesis 1:26-27 tells us that human beings are made in the "image of God." Humans do not grow into the image of God or attain it in adulthood; the text says "Let Us make man in Our image." Henry (2010) states that Christ is the only express image of God, but human beings made in the image of God consist of three things:

1. In the nature and constitution of God's soul, not a physical body, our soul portrays the clearest image of God in our understanding, will, and active power.
2. God's authority is given to humans to have dominion over other creatures as well as their own will, which means humans are His representatives on earth.
3. God's justice and purity are displayed in the knowledge, righteousness, and true holiness granted to Adam and Eve (pp. 4-5).

In Genesis 5:3, Adam becomes a father after 130 years of life. The Scripture says that "...he [Adam] became the father of a son in his own likeness, according to his image..." (NASB), which indicates that Adam and now humans are the vessel through which further images of God are created. All children, regardless of race, gender, or social status, are created in the image of God, which gives them a special value for both God and the world (Fretheim, 2008, p. 4). That special value is one major reason educators must seriously consider curricula to which children are exposed. Children should be taught with resources that glorify God and the church, but haphazardly choosing these curriculum resources will not bring glory to God.

Aside from being created in God's image, children are considered a blessing from the beginning. In Genesis 1:26-28 and in Psalm 128:1-4, children are a part of the blessing given to those who choose to follow God (May, Posterski, Stonehouse, & Cannell, 2005, p. 27). The Hebrews viewed children as gifts from God. In Genesis 48:9, Genesis 33:5, and Joshua 24:3-4, we find Jacob referring to the children who "God has graciously given...." The Psalms depict children as sources of joy (113:9), and in Psalm 127:3-5, it is stated that many sons bring delight. God intended children as a blessing for all (May et al., 2005, p. 28).

Children were not only a general blessing, but they were also at the core of the covenant with Abraham in Genesis 12. After the fall of Adam and Eve, God called Abraham into a covenant relationship with Him. God promised Abraham that He would make a great nation from his descendants. The first child born under the covenant was Isaac, and Abraham's faithfulness to God after Isaac's birth proved to be a blessing (May et al., 2005, p. 19). The blessing coming through children was a choice by God. God is sovereign, and He chose for the blessing to be fulfilled through children. God validated the worth of children through this decision.

Children and Instruction in the Old Testament

Much is found in Deuteronomy regarding children and the teaching of children. Meaning *second law*, Deuteronomy is viewed as polity or a constitution, which indicates it is foundational for life for God's people

(Miller, 2008, p. 46). Moses is believed to have authored Deuteronomy, and Moses' role in Deuteronomy is that of teaching or instructing, which creates a second purpose of Deuteronomy—teaching. Deuteronomy is not only important in its content but in its structure too (Miller, 2008, p. 46).

Deuteronomy instructs the Israelites on the education and training of children. When talking about children, Miller (2008) makes a much-needed distinction: does the word *children* refer to age or a relationship, or even possibly, to both? Deuteronomy 1:39 refers to the "little ones" and "your children who today do not yet know right from wrong." The word for children, *taph*, means children or little children and appears 42 times in the New American Standard Bible (NASB) (Taph, n.d.). Both words indicate that both age and relationship are important to the understanding of Deuteronomy (Miller, 2008, pp. 47-48). The use of the word *children* in the Scripture is applicable to the value of the physical child and the value of the mindset of the child in relation to God. Ryken, Wilhoit, and Longman (1998) state that of more than 500 references to child and children in the Bible, approximately half are considered literal references (p. 141).

In Deuteronomy 4:9-10 and 31:12-13, Moses speaks of the need to teach the younger generation. They have not been exposed to the teaching of the history of Israel and the Law; therefore, Moses is commanding that it be done, which indicates the necessity for all to know what has come previously. In these two passages, Moses indicates that the next generation is to be taught the story of the giving of the commandments on the mountain and that they are to regularly recite the laws throughout time so future generations will also know. Children are to know the laws and pass them on to future generations (Miller, 2008, pp. 49-50). People were not merely to know the laws, but they were also to follow them. The word fear in these verses, "Assemble the people to Me, that I may let them hear My words so they may learn to fear Me all the days they live on the earth, and that they may teach their children," (NASB) comes from the Hebrew word *yare*, which actually means "to stand in awe of, reverence, honor, respect." According to Vines (1996), *yare* can be used to refer to an exalted person. It is not ordinary fear but a reverence, which results in respect. It is suggested the word implies submission ethically to God. This fear goes beyond the psychological reaction of fear (pp. 79-80). Out of that reverence and awe

comes the obedience to the laws. Moses was concerned with the generation before him and the generations to come.

It is important to realize that Deuteronomy 6 is addressed to Israel not
just families. Children will and do observe all of the people in their community. God's plan in Deuteronomy 6 is for the entire faith community to
support the family and children. God hopes that children will see many
adults living obediently for God (May et al., 2005, p. 34). McIntosh (2002,
p. 89) believes the effectiveness of parents' teaching on their children is not
seen in just the behavior of the child. The goal of their teaching should
be not just merely to keep the next generation alive, but that faith in and
obedience to God would always be kept alive. McIntosh aptly brings to
light that if a church cannot help its own children come to faith in God,
then how can that church think they will have an impact on others outside
of the church. God does not place the responsibility for the rearing of children solely on the parents. The entire church is to be prepared to instruct
the younger generation whether it is through example or direct instruction.
Parents entrust some of the instruction of their children to others in the
church. Curriculum is a foundational tool for such instruction, and it must
be chosen carefully to ensure children are instructed properly and with
faithfulness to God's word.

Moses also addresses the aim of instruction, which is the same for
children and adults. According to Miller (2008, p. 53), the first and main
goal of teaching is that all would learn to fear the Lord (Deuteronomy
4:10, 6:1-2, 14:23, 17:19, 31:12-13). It is the intention that through obser-
vance of the law, fear of the Lord will be developed. The goal of the law
is obedience, but also a proper relationship with the Lord (Miller, 2008, p.
53). Stonehouse (1998, p. 25) refers to Deuteronomy 6:2 to suggest that
the goal of teaching is to develop faith in God passed through generations. Children are to develop a healthy fear of the Lord, which results in
a deeper faith in Him.

In Deuteronomy 6:6-9, Moses articulates how children are to be instructed. Children were to be taught these commands not only at home,
but everywhere (Kalland, 1992, p. 65). In verses 4-9, Moses focuses on
one's relationship with God. Verses 4-6 indicate three elements of a life
obedient to God: 1) people need to know God, 2) people are to be obedient out of love for God, and 3) people need to internalize God's laws and

meditate on them so His laws will become an internal guiding force, not a set of restrictions. These elements will help followers teach because obedience out of love results in others being drawn to that love (May et al., 2005, p. 33).

Repeating laws everywhere is to benefit not only one's family, but friends and companions as well (Henry, n.d., p. 752). The Hebrew word for "impress" in the New International Version (NIV) is from the root *sanan*, which can mean, "repeat, say again, or second time" (Kalland, 1992, p. 65). In the NASB, the verse says, "You shall teach them diligently." The Hebrew words for both teach and *diligently* are *shanan*, meaning "to sharpen or to whet" ("Deuteronomy 6:6-9," n.d.). Henry (n.d.) suggests that these laws are to be repeated in hopes they will perpetuate themselves in the future (p. 752). A picture of one etching words onto a stone monument is given by Merrill (1994, p. 167). A chisel and hammer are used to etch a saying into stone with great care and effort, and once done, the message stays. Merrill relates this process to the desire Moses expresses in these verses for the generations to come to have the word of God "etched" into them. May et al. (2005) believes that verse 7 indicates adults were to teach the commandments in the "flow" of life. Conversations about the laws were not to merely be formal, but a natural and integral part of life (p. 33). Spiritual training opportunities were and are to be fully seized. Whether it is formally talking about the commandments, informally displaying them "as you walk along the road," late in the day "when you lie down" or early "when you get up," they are to be seized. Moses uses a literary term, *merism*, which means to use two extremes to suggest everything in between. From formal to informal, early to late, Israel and the church today are to be involved in the spiritual training of the younger generations (McIntosh, 2002, p. 86). The hyperbole used in this passage encompasses all human effort and the entire span of time, which is to be centered on the teaching of the truths of the Lord (Merrill, 1994, p. 167).

Verses 8 and 9 refer to placing the commandments as symbols by tying them to hands and foreheads. Kalland suggests that this is to be taken metaphorically and spiritually due to the nature of a similar metaphor in Exodus 13:9-16 when the firstborn is said to be like a sign on the hand or forehead (Kalland, 1992, pp. 65-66). Henry (n.d.) suggests that at the time of Deuteronomy there were very few copies of the law; therefore, important Scriptures were to be written on walls and scrolls to assist in providing them with a constant reminder of the law (p. 752). May et al. (2005) believes the symbols were to introduce the laws, but true understanding comes by seeing it lived out (p. 33). These verses are the basis of the Jewish custom of placing Scriptures (the Torah; Deuteronomy 6:4-9 and Deuteronomy 11:13-21) in a small box, called the *mezuzah*, on door frames (Merrill, 1994, p. 168). Even today, man is to make the laws of the Lord a constant presence in life. Beyond symbolism, these commands were to be mental constraints on people. These symbols demonstrate that God's law was to be infused into everyday matters of life, and His authority was over all things (McIntosh, 2002, p. 87). Either way, children were to be taught not only the ideal, but also how to live each day.

Throughout the Bible, the emphasis placed on child-bearing is evident. On occasions, children were given names to remind people of God's desires. Isaiah was given two children whom he named Shear-Jashub, meaning, "a remnant will return," and Maher-Shalal-Hash-Baz, meaning, "quick to the plunder, swift to the spoil." God told Isaiah, in Isaiah 7:3—8:3, to give his boys these names in order to help convey God's message to the nation of Judah (Zuck, 1996, pp. 45-46). God used children in this instance to further His ministry.

Children and Instruction in the New Testament

Moving to the New Testament, the greatest teachings found concerning children are Jesus' view of children. The very first point to note is the incarnation of Christ. God's covenant with Abraham could not be fulfilled through the law; a new covenant was needed as seen in Jeremiah 31:31. This new covenant began with the birth of a baby, not with an adult. John 1:14 demonstrates that the new covenant meant God had to come and live among us to show us grace. He did not come as an adult; instead, He came as a child, lived all phases of childhood, and became an adult. The incarnation supports the significance of children (May et al., 2005, p. 38).

Reading through the Gospels does not present many examples of teaching directly to or involving children, but it must be considered that the culture at that time did not promote the presence of children. Given cultural considerations, the presence of children in the life of Jesus is actually prominent. Under the leadership of the Holy Spirit, all three Synoptic Gospels included Jesus' teaching on children:

1. Matthew 18:1-5; Mark 9:33-37; Luke 9:46-48—Jesus set a child in the middle of the disciples as a symbol of humility and greatness.
2. Matthew 18:6-16; Mark 9:41-48; Luke 17:1-2—Jesus warns of causing a child to stumble.
3. Matthew 19:13-15; Mark 10:13-16; Luke 18:15-17—Jesus blesses the children.

The book of John excludes the teaching of the children in his "Good News," but children are used metaphorically for entering a relationship with God in John 3:3-6 (May et al., 2005, p. 39). An analysis of Jesus' interaction with children will provide a deeper understanding of the value of the "little ones."

Matthew 18:1-5; Mark 9:33-37; Luke 9:46-48

These passages in the Synoptic Gospels are both similar and different as with most passages in the Synoptic Gospels. In all three passages, Jesus addresses the disciples who were asking about the greatest in God's kingdom. Jesus answered them in all three by placing a child before them and explaining that to welcome a child in His name was the same as welcoming Him. The word translated as child in all three passages is *paidion*, which means a young child, an infant just born or child-like in intellect. *Paidion* appears 52 times in the NASB ("Matthew 18:1-5," n.d.). Matthew says that Jesus called a child to Him, and Mark and Luke wrote that Jesus "took" a little child. Matthew and Mark say Jesus had the child "stand among them," and Luke says the child "stood beside Jesus." Mark adds that Jesus took the child in His arms; therefore, the assumption from all three Synoptic Gospels is that Jesus called the child, placed the child beside him facing the disciples, and then set the child on His lap. Matthew then adds that Jesus made a statement that in order to enter the kingdom of heaven you must become like little children. Mark and Luke include this statement, but in separate passages when Jesus rebukes the disciples for sending children away from Him (Zuck, 1996, pp. 204-211). Jesus chose to use children as examples in His teaching, and the example, in and of itself, suggests significance.

In this important account in Scripture, the story portrayed is meaningful for the lives of both adults and children. In Matthew 18, the disciples argue as to who is the greatest, and Jesus settles the argument by bringing forth a child and saying in verses 3-4, "Truly I tell you, unless you change and become like little children, you will never enter the kingdom of heaven. Therefore, whoever takes a humble place—becoming like this child—is the greatest in the kingdom of heaven." Jesus does not command us to be like adults in our relationship to Him; instead, He says we are to be like a child in our relationship to Him (White, 2008, p. 364). Ryken, Wilhoit, and Longman (1998) suggest it is the child's teachable attitude that Christ wants adults to model.

Carson (1984, pp. 396-397) believes that the child is used as an ideal of humility and disregard for social status, but does not believe the child is used as an example of innocence, purity, or faith. Jesus is promoting humility of mind, not child-like thought (Carson, 1984, p. 397). The very question the disciples asked demonstrated a serious lack of understanding. The disciples were assuming God's kingdom would be like other kingdoms where status and rank were the requirements for greatness (Weber, 2000, p. 286). The use of children is indeed metaphorical, but the mere idea of using a child as a metaphor indicates importance. According to Henry (2010) Christ took a child and used him so adults could learn from the child; therefore, adults should not consider children unworthy company (p. 1489). A metaphor is a literary device to teach or to give an example, and Jesus would not just select anything for this metaphor—He chose a child to demonstrate the attitude needed to obtain the Kingdom of Heaven.

Matthew 18:6-16; Mark 9:41-48; Luke 17:1-2

Aside from emphasizing the value and the mindset of children, Christ also warned against hindering a child. In Matthew 18:6-7, Mark 9:42, and Luke 17:1-2, Jesus expresses that hindering a child on their spiritual journey would be a serious offense, which should result in death by drowning. The Greek word for child in all three passages is *mikros*, which appears a total of 46 times in the NASB. *Mikros* is translated as small or little of size, space, age, time, quantity, or rank ("Mikros," n.d.).

Verse 6 of Matthew 18 states, "but whoever causes one of these little ones who believe in Me to stumble, it would be better for him to have a heavy millstone hung around his neck, and to be drowned in the depth of the sea" (NASB). It was better that a person be put to death by drowning rather than deceiving, leading astray, or setting a bad example for a child. A millstone was sometimes attached by a rope to the neck of a donkey in order to help women turn slabs of stone to grind grain. This large stone tied to the donkey's neck was so large it would be impossible to escape drowning if such a stone was tied to a person's neck. The Greek word for stumble in this passage is *skandalizo*, which translates as to entice to sin ("Skandalizo," n.d.). This example shows not only the extreme danger in leading a child astray but also Jesus' love and value for the little ones (Zuck, 1996, p. 210). Weber (2000) states that Jesus' punishment of the one who influenced a new believer to sin is greater than the punishment of the one who sins. The one influencing has greater responsibility, therefore, harsher punishment. The imagery used in the passage demonstrates this responsibility. If a believer puts a stumbling block in the path of a new believer, then a contrasting huge millstone is placed around the elder believer's neck leading to drowning in the sea. Jesus could have said the same stone would be placed around the elder believer's neck, and he would be drowned in a few feet of water; instead, the use of a millstone and a drowning in the depths of the sea was used to demonstrate the severity of this action (Weber, 2000, p. 288). Christ was alluding to new believers in this passage, but children who are young believers are not excluded. If children were of no value, then why would He care if they were hindered? This passage is a major reason a leader must select curriculum carefully—curriculum can easily hinder a child if not chosen properly.

The above story is mentioned in all three Synoptic gospels though at different places chronologically. Matthew includes it with the story of welcoming a little child in Matthew 18, but Mark and Luke place it later in Scripture (Zuck, 1996, p. 210). In the prior verse, verse 5, Matthew presents Jesus' promise about receiving a child and verse 6 follows with the warning to not cause little ones to sin. There is debate regarding what is meant by the words, "welcoming a little child like this," but Zuck presents that since the little child was on Jesus' lap when He said these words, it seems Jesus meant literally both children and adult followers.

In Matthew 18:10, Jesus commands not to look down on the "little ones." So previously, Jesus warns against leading children astray, and now He goes further and says adults are not to even look down on or think negatively towards children (White, 2008, pp. 364-365). These verses once again emphasize humility in attitude for followers of Christ (Carson, 1984, pp. 399-401). Jesus is emphasizing the importance of children once more.

Matthew 19:13-15; Mark 10:13-16; Luke 18:15-17

Children were constantly brought to Jesus for Him to bless, but in their human nature, the disciples felt children were a bother to Jesus. This is the only occurrence in the New Testament where Jesus is recorded as being indignant (Weber, 1979, p. 15). Jesus displays anger when He clears the temple of money changers, but the word indignant or rebuke is not used in this instance. In all three Synoptic Gospels, the incident of the disciples sending the children away from Jesus and Jesus' reply of indignation is recorded, and all three are surrounded by a story about humility. *Paidion* is again the Greek word used in these passages ("Matthew 19:13-15," n.d.). Luke 18 does include *paidion* with the addition of the Greek word *brephos* for babies, which is translated as an unborn child, a newborn child, or an infant (Vines, 1996 p. 48). All three Synoptic passages are followed by the story of the rich young man who did not recognize his helplessness. The passages in Matthew and Mark are placed after instructions regarding marriage and divorce. The passage in Luke follows the story of the tax collector who humbled himself before God. Zuck believes that the placement of the story of the children in the midst of stories of humility emphasizes the need for childlike faith in God (1996, p. 216).

In these passages, Jesus clearly states, "Let the little children come to me" (White, 2008, p. 364). Not only did Christ have the children return to Him, but He also went on to use them as an illustration of the trust needed for salvation (Zuck, 1996, p. 213). According to Zuck, this incident indicates several things for people today: parents should bring their children to Christ, Jesus is not too busy for children, Jesus loves children, Jesus desires for children's ministries to grow, God's kingdom includes both children and adults who come to Christ in a sense of humility, and finally, children are our model for how to receive God's kingdom.

The passage does not indicate who brought the children. Perhaps brothers, sisters, or fathers, but it is these that the disciples rebuked. The Scriptures do not say why the disciples did not feel the children should come to Jesus—unclean, undignified? Nonetheless, the disciples were surprised when Christ responded harshly to their own actions instead of to the children. Weber (1979) stated, "Indeed, it is in such extraordinary actions and sayings in the midst of everyday scenes of life with seemingly unimportant people like women and children that the very core of the Gospel is revealed" (p. 17).

As Jesus took the children in His arms, He symbolized the gift of the kingdom of God. The children did not earn this—the text only suggests the helplessness and weakness of the children. Nothing is stated in regard to the children being innocent or possessing childlike confidence. Weber believes the main point of this passage is not the nature of the children, but the nature of God. In Matthew 5:3, children are considered among the "poor in spirit," and Jesus' love for children is as unreasonable as the generosity of the steward in the parable of the laborers in the vineyard in Matthew 20:1-2. This love of children counters Greek and Jewish classifications, and applying human terms to God's kingdom would give children a place of preeminence (Weber, 1979, p. 19). Henry (2010) notes that Christ received the children. The action was taken by Him to reach down to them. Believers do not take hold of Christ, He takes hold of them, and even small children who cannot reach out their own arms are capable of being taken hold of by Christ (p. 1496).

Jesus' method of teaching in this passage is an indication of the New Testament culture. Jesus lived in an oral culture, and often actions and sayings were tied together. He did just that in this instance as well as at the Last Supper. The teaching through words and the illustrations complement each other and communicate the message together more memorably.

Overall, Mark 10 records that the kingdom of God belongs to children, which means they are valued members of any community. Jesus also spent time with the children and gave them individual attention not always afforded to adults. Jesus also used children as an example to teach adults (White, 2008, p. 354). Zuck (1996) points out that Christ loved children, spent time with them, and ministered to them so as to remind church leaders that if children are neglected, then the example set by Christ is being neglected.

The Scriptures validate that children are created by God and are instruments for His work. As leaders, teachers, and ministers, there is responsibility for training and instructing these children to love Christ. The responsibility is great and involves making choices, including curriculum. The Holy Spirit is what allows children to grow spiritually, but it is the responsibility of teachers, leaders, and ministers to provide an environment, including curriculum, that allows the Holy Spirit to work. It is this biblical support for the value of children and role of the Holy Spirit that attests to the vital role played by those choosing curriculum resources in the church. It is a choice that must be guided by the Holy Spirit and evaluated in more ways than finances and ease of use. Those in this role should approach this decision with great care, evaluation, and prayer. God's Word does not dismiss the instruction of children and nor should church leaders.

References

Carson, D. A. (1984). Matthew. In F. E. Gxbelein (Ed.), *The expositor's Bible commentary with the New International Version: Matthew, Mark, Luke Volume 8* (pp. 3-602). Grand Rapids, MI: Zondervan.

Fretheim, T. E. (2008). "God was with the boy" (Genesis 21:20); Children in the book of Genesis. In M. J. Bunge (ed.), *The child in the Bible* (pp. 3-23). Grand Rapids, MI: William B. Eerdmans.

Henry, M. (n.d.). *Matthew Henry's commentary on the whole Bible: Vol 1. Genesis to Deuteronomy.* McLean, VA: MacDonald.

Henry, M. (2010). *The new Matthew Henry commentary: The Classic work with updated language.* Edited by M. H. Manser. Grand Rapids, MI: Zondervan.

Kalland, E. S. (1992). Deuteronomy. In F. E. Gxbelein (Ed.), *The expositor's Bible commentary with the New International Version: Deuteronomy, Joshua, Judges, Ruth, 1 & 2 Samuel Volume 3* (pp. 3-238). Grand Rapids, MI: Zondervan.

McIntosh, D. (2002). *Holman Old Testament commentary: Deuteronomy.* Nashville, TN: B & H.

Matthew 18:1-5. (n.d.). In Biblestudytools.com. Retrieved from http://www. biblestudytools.com/interlinear-bible/passage.aspx?q=matthew +18%3A1-5&t=nas

Matthew 19:13-15. (n.d.). In Biblestudytools.com. Retrieved from http:// www.biblestudytools.com/interlinear-bible/passage.aspx?q=matthew +19:13-15&t=nas

May, S., Posterski, B., Stonehouse, C., & Cannell, L. (2005). *Children matter: Celebrating their place in the church, family, and community.* Grand Rapids, MI: William B. Eerdmans.

Merrill, E. H. (1994). *The new American commentary: An evangelical and theological exposition of Holy Scriptures, Deuteronomy.* Nashville, TN: B & H.

Mikros. (n.d.). In Biblestudytools.com. Retrieved from http://www.biblestudytools.com/lexicons/greek/nas/mikros.html

Miller, P. D. (2008). That the children may know: Children in Deuteronomy. In M. J. Bunge (ed.), *The child in the Bible* (pp. 45-62). Grand Rapids, MI: William B. Eerdmans.

Ryken, L., Wilhoit, J. C., & Longman, T. (Eds.). (1998). *Dictionary of biblical imagery.* Downers Grove, IL: InterVarsity Press.

Skandalizo. (n.d.) In Biblestudytools.com. Retrieved from http://www.biblestudytools.com/lexicons/greek/nas/skandalizo.html

Stonehouse, C. (1998). *Joining children on the spiritual journey: Nurturing a life of faith.* Grand Rapids, MI: BridgePoint Books.

Vines, W. E. (1996). *Vine's complete expository dictionary of Old and New Testament words.* Nashville, TN: Thomas Nelson.

Weber, H. R. (1979). *Jesus and the children: Biblical resources for study and preaching.* Geneva, Switzerland: World Council of Churches.

Weber, S. K. (2000). *Holman New Testament commentary: Matthew.* Nashville, TN: B & H.

White, K. J. (2008). "He placed a little child in the midst": Jesus, the kingdom, and children. In M. J. Bunge (ed.), *The child in the Bible* (pp. 353-374). Grand Rapids, MI: William B. Eerdmans.

Zuck, R. B. (1996). *Precious in His sight: Childhood and children in the Bible.* Grand Rapids, MI: Baker Books.

Author Biography

Dr. Amanda Cooley is the Camp Director for Grey Stone Kids Camp (Grey Stone Church, Durham) and an Instructor of Christian Education in the Baptist Women's Institute of Southeastern Baptist Theological Seminary in Wake Forest, North Carolina. In her spare time she also works for Apple, Inc.

Parents Can Be the Church's Ministry Multipliers

Ron Hunter Jr.

Discipleship can be described mathematically with a rather odd looking fraction. The 1/168 fraction presents a tough number to visualize. To grasp this tiny number, one should try cutting a round pie or cake into one hundred sixty-eight equal pieces. This denominator stands for the number of hours in a week. The alarming part is what the numerator (one) represents: the average number of hours a person spends in discipleship each week. This figure comes from thirty minutes of teaching received in a life group, small group, or class and another thirty minutes of listening to the senior pastor or student pastor. One's response should be, "It is not enough."

If an adult or child receives on average only one hour of spiritual influence per week, how does a church acquire more opportunities to provide coaching or instruction? The primary way to multiply student or children's ministry is by getting parents involved during the family's time at home. Recent decades have shown less time is spent at church with fewer services. Staff is spending most efforts planning the one main attendance time that typically includes a main service and a small group setting (worship and discipleship). Discipleship is "the process of devoting oneself to learn from and become more like them [Christ]" (Mangum, 2014). This type of devotion and followership cannot occur in one to three hours a week. Discipleship has to be part of everyday life and the numerator must become a larger number. This research shows the biblical expectation of parental involvement in discipleship as well the influence parents provide their kids to challenge the current culture of expecting the church to be the sole equipping or discipling source.

Power of Parental Influence

If the church only gets an hour of discipleship in during the two hours people spend at church, then the home is the next logical, and biblical, place to target. Parents can be the church's greatest ministry multipliers. One can immediately recognize the amount of influence parents have on children. Infants crawl until finally pulling up beside the couch, let go with one hand and turn toward the middle of the room—risking it all and letting go, one step, two steps, and plop, fall. The little one looks up from this crumpled position to see the parent's reaction—what they did, what they said, and how they looked—to *interpret the moment*. If Mom seemed scared or upset, the crying commenced. If Mom cheered or clapped, the laughing began. Through the developmental years and into adolescence, children interpret the world through parents' reactions.

Why do grown kids support college football teams when their parents moved the family away from that state when the kids were just five and six? They cheer, wear the colors, and watch faithfully because their Mom and Dad do. Their grandparents often have the same influence. The kids caught the spirit and became fans because of the influence of family. From outside observations (say a visiting international guest), one could easily believe college football is the religion of choice.

From their earliest moments, kids take their cues from their parents. Parents provide, especially in the early childhood developmental years, "the comprehensive framework of one's basic beliefs about things" (Wolters, 2005, p. 2). Hunter (Hunter, 2010, p. 6) citing Colson (1999) defined worldview as "the sum total of our beliefs about the world, the 'big picture' that directs our daily decisions and actions...[it] is a way of seeing and comprehending *all* reality" (pp. 14-15). Parents are largely responsible for the early development of their child's worldview. They are later influenced by others, but never to the same degree as by the core values taught by dads and moms. Parents inspire and shape their child's desires and gripes. Into their teen years and beyond, kids tend to laugh at what parents laugh at and fear what parents fear. Their root attitudes come from watching how Dad and Mom interpret life.

Kids and grown kids often view the following items similar or opposite to the views of their parents: money, politics, authority, education, sports, race, religion, death, and holidays. The power and legacy of family influence runs deep and touches multiple areas. If parents respect law enforcement and authority figures, the kids will honor positions and titles. Parents determine how a child manages money: whether or not they budget and how they deal with debt or savings. Parents' routines around the holidays determine if gifts are opened on Christmas Eve or Day, if birthdays are a big deal, and if the family must endure the Macy's Thanksgiving Day Parade. If dad and mom value education; read to their kids; and do not discount math, science, or history, then the child will probably be a good student with great likelihood to complete undergrad and possibly graduate work. Parents' values prompt attitudes, actions, and accomplishments.

The context of Scripture is clear: God defines *family* as generations of dads and moms influencing their children and grandchildren. He designed and talked about the ideal home as having a dad and mom loving one or more children in the way He, our heavenly Father, loves us (Genesis 2, Deuteronomy 6, Ephesians 6, Psalm 103:13). He intends parents to coach their kids toward spiritual growth so they in turn will do the same for their kids.

Society does not provide the ideal for families. It was never God's desire for marriages to end in divorce, and yet throughout Scripture, He used and blessed single moms. The family is not always an ideal set of parents and kids all doing what God intended. The Bible reminds of adapted models of generational discipleship. The often quoted and normal secession of teaching flows from father to son and on to grandson as seen in Abraham, Isaac, and Jacob. There is not always a godly father or mother as evidenced in Mordecai teaching his niece, Esther and (Titus 1:4) Paul mentoring his adopted son in the faith, Titus. Timothy's faithful mother seemed to carry the whole spiritual parental influence. Regardless of what season of life, God can use a person to teach someone in their family or someone adopted by way of friendships and connections.

Traditional: Abraham, Isaac, Jacob
Related: Mordecai, Esther
One Parent: Eunice, Timothy
Adopted: Paul, Titus

By default and for a myriad of reasons, grandparents sometimes raise their grandchildren. The vital truth to remember is God wants the church to help shape the home—even if broken or damaged—into what He intends. The term "parents" in this paper may suggest a dad and mom, stepparents, a single dad, a single mom, adoptive parents, or grandparents.

Generational Power

Does this premise hold up biblically? One of the genealogies frequently noted in Scripture is Abraham, Isaac, and Jacob. What did the sons learn from the fathers? Although these biblical greats are most known for their roles as the patriarchs of the nation of Israel, they were far from perfect, and each father passed along character flaws to his son. A small thread of deception grew when Abraham lied about Sarah being his wife by claiming her as his sister (Genesis 20). His son Isaac later faced a similar situation (Genesis 26). Like his dad, he lied about Rebekah, his wife, suggesting she was his sister to preserve his own well-being. When Isaac's son was born, the name he received described the person he was: Jacob—heel catcher, supplanter (one taking the place of another), and trickster or deceiver.

This trickster took advantage of his older brother twice. When his brother, Esau, was weak, hungry, and desperate, Jacob conned him out of his birthright by coercing him to trade it for a mess of pottage. But the worst deception was the second one, when he deceived his almost-blind father by pretending to be his brother and stealing Esau's blessing. Jacob's accomplice? His mom. His model? His dad. Jacob, his dad, and his grand-dad all lied to get something they wanted—what an inheritance! Dysfunction is not limited to current culture.

Another recognizable genealogy shows how womanizing and misplaced priorities were passed from David to Solomon and on to Rehoboam. The passages outlining the Ten Commandments discuss the implications of generations, specifically the Exodus 20 narrative and the following generational verses: Exodus 20:5-6, 10, and 12. Deuteronomy 5 also reiterates the Ten Commandments. Deuteronomy 5:9-10, 14, 16, and 29 leads into the foundational passage of Deuteronomy 6:5-9, the *Shema*, the same one dedicated Jews quote each morning. The *Shema* does not emphasize the rules of the Ten Commandments, but rather what parents should pass along to their kids: how Dad and Mom love God and love His Word enough to make it a part of their daily life. Deuteronomy 6 speaks to parents in the same way Proverbs 1:8 speaks to children. Both emphasize an instructional relationship.

A parent should never underestimate the influence of the previous generation. Genesis 18:19 calls parents to instruct kids and live out a consistent relationship with the Lord. Exodus 12:26-27 and 13:14-15 show how Dad and Mom can point out the presence of God and His power within a family. This helps kids build trust in Him for their future. Seven hundred years later, God says the same thing in Isaiah 38:19. Going forward nearly another eight hundred years, Paul reaches back to the faith of Timothy's grandparents (2 Timothy 1:3-5) when instructing him about the faith-legacy of his ancestors.

Because parents do not naturally assume this role, the church must show them how to do it. Dads, with the right instruction, can tell the story of the way God's intervention, sustaining power, strength, wisdom, or other presence helped at a significant life junction. With the right tools, the family's perspective on God's involvement will go beyond major events. Parents bring the reality and influence of God into the home by showing the kids how to follow Him rather than charting just any course on their own. A leader's task is to help parents see that the family challenge is not a new one and that God prescribed a solution from the beginning.

Daniel, Shadrach, Meshach, and Abednego cheered for the God of their parents even when living in a foreign land. Kids cheer for the parent's college team, and tend to value what the parents value—good or bad. College football is not all there is in this world. Parents need to emphasize and cheer for God the way they cheer for their teams. The team jerseys, players, stats, opponents, and even the time set aside to spend in this worship (yes, that word is intentional) each week. What if parents apply the same devotion to God?

Generational Discipleship in Scripture

God spoke about the power of generational discipleship not only in Deuteronomy 6, but throughout Scripture. He began making His intention clear at the time of creation, when He told Adam and Eve to "Be fruitful and multiply and fill the earth" (Genesis 1:28, English Standard Version, ESV). The command is repeated because it is not limited to physical procreation. As noted in the genealogies found in Genesis 5, the Earth grew very populated, and yet God showed His disappointment in this "multiplied" people because they were not following Him. The flood allowed a do-over, and God spoke to Noah's family, saying again, "Be fruitful" (Genesis 9:1, 7). It seems clear that population alone was not the goal or the world would have a prediluvian success. The essence of His intent was *multiply My presence on this earth through your children.*

The generational thread winds its way throughout the Old and New Testaments. God told the patriarch Abraham, father of the nation of Israel, that he should direct his children and family in righteousness and justice (Genesis 18:19). Moses instructed the family leaders to be able to answer their children's questions by showing how God's involvement in everyday life has purpose and meaning (Deuteronomy 6:20-25). In Isaiah 38:19, seven hundred years later, Hezekiah described how each generation will define God's greatness based upon what the previous one has taught.

After the fall of Judah and Israel, God still focused on generations passing along their faith and values during the rebuilding of Jerusalem. The great leader and contractor of the wall, Nehemiah, worked quickly to complete his building project, but called a time-out to talk to the leaders of the families. When the wall was half-built and the enemy was threatening and mocking their God, he said, "Do not be afraid of them. Remember the Lord, who is great and awesome, and fight for your brothers, your sons, your daughters, your wives, and your homes" (Nehemiah 4:14, ESV). What a powerful command for parents today!

The family theme flows seamlessly through every age from Old to New Testaments. The Old Testament closes with a generational exclamation point in Malachi 4:6, showing God's desire to turn the hearts of the fathers to be in tune with their children and vice versa so each will follow God. Interestingly, events of the New Testament opens with Elizabeth hearing what John the Baptist, her future son, would do. Luke 1:17 describes how he will "turn the hearts of the fathers to the children." The principles of generational discipleship appear consistently throughout Scripture for all people. And they still apply today—even if parents, like the generations of Nehemiah, have forgotten to be spiritual leaders to their kids.

The New Testament quotes Deuteronomy, Psalms, and Isaiah more than any other books in the Old Testament (VanderKam, 1994). Jesus quoted from the twin pillars of Deuteronomy 6:5 and Leviticus 19:18, summarizing them into two commands (Christensen, 2001; Woods, 2011): "And he said to him, 'You shall love the Lord your God with all your heart and with all your soul and with all your mind. This is the great and first commandment. And a second is like it: You shall love your neighbor as yourself. On these two commandments depend all the Law and the Prophets' " (Matthew 22:37-40, ESV). To suggest Deuteronomy is outdated or limit it to ancient Israel would overlook how often the words of Jesus, Paul, and the New Testament as a whole reference this foundational book in general and this passage in particular.

From Generation to Generation

Church leaders must constantly look for better ways to equip parents so they, in turn, can coach their kids. The philosophy of Deuteronomy 6 comes from ancient roots found in the way God instructed Hebrew parents to be leaders in their kids' lives. From the very beginning, God wanted the tabernacle, and later the temple, to be the center of life around which people built their homes (or pitched their tents). Homes or tents surrounded the tabernacle in distinct fan-like sections according to their tribes, indicating that when God moves the church, the people respond by moving as well.

God's intent has always been a close-knit church leading and parents teaching one generation after another. The core Deuteronomy 6 passage shows parents how to allow their love for God and His Word to overflow into the lives of their kids and let a Christ-following relationship be caught and taught:

Now this is the commandment—the statutes and the rules—that the LORD your God commanded me to teach you, that you may do them in the land to which you are going over, to possess it, that you may fear the LORD your God, you and your son and your son's son, by keeping all his statutes and his commandments, which I command you, all the days of your life, and that your days may be long. Hear therefore, O Israel, and be careful to do them, that it may go well with you, and that you may multiply greatly, as the LORD, the God of your fathers, has promised you, in a land flowing with milk and honey.

Hear, O Israel: The LORD our God, the LORD is one. You shall love the LORD your God with all your heart and with all your soul and with all your might. And these words that I command you today shall be on your heart. You shall teach them diligently to your children, and shall talk of them when you sit in your house, and when you walk by the way, and when you lie down, and when you rise. You shall bind them as a sign on your hand, and they shall be as frontlets between your eyes. You shall write them on the doorposts of your house and on your gates.

Deuteronomy 6:1-9 (emphasis on verses 4-7, ESV)

This passage shares God's *command*, not suggestion. God intended it to describe an educational process for families to disciple each generation. Deuteronomy 6 instructed the entire nation about how their faith and values could reach their great-grandchildren. These few verses shaped the lineage of Israel and still have the ability to shape culture today. At heart, this command tells parents to love God, love His Word, and teach their kids to do the same. The best lessons come from natural interactions during everyday life, much the way Jesus used parables to teach His disciples. Deuteronomy 6 asks parents to look for teachable moments throughout the day to help their kids adopt and own what they model as adults. Home is where most kids form habits. Deuteronomy 6 is about changing the heart of parents to change their homes and thereby shaping the habits of their kids.

Reciprocal Relationships

The New Testament sibling passage to Deuteronomy 6 is Ephesians 6, and the parallels are stunning. Paul begins this chapter with additional commentary on the commandment to honor your father and mother. In recalling the Ten Commandments that were so familiar to New Testament believers, Paul noted that the command to obey your parents requires a reciprocal relationship. Dads and moms expect honor, respect, and obedience from children. But Paul reminded parents, specifically dads, that to receive honor, they must likewise be careful not to consistently agitate or anger their kids but carefully nurture a relationship.

The church should teach parents how to intentionally build relationships filled with grace. Dads provide a model for kids, who often derive their view of the heavenly Father by what they know and experience with their earthly father. Deuteronomy 6 and Ephesians 6 expect dads (and moms) to build healthy relationships with their children and teens.

The Ephesians passage also discusses critical issues for family relationships. Paul taught the New Testament believers a code of conduct for the home where the relational connections emanate from emotional ties, and anger issues push kids farther from the parents and from the heavenly Father (Lincoln, 1990). Paul spoke of parental anger and how it can discourage kids in Ephesians 4:29, as well as in Colossians 3:20-21.

The church should help parents recognize that the heavenly Father loans their children to them for a season (Psalm 127:3-5, Deuteronomy 6, Ephesians 6:4). Like good stewards, parents must increase their kids' self-worth to line up with their actual worth as God determines it. Parents cannot go about this process alone, but will need the help of the church and specific individuals such as lead pastors, children's ministers, youth ministers, grandparents, aunts, and other special people who will champion and reinforce the biblical teachings through godly relationships.

Negative Generational Impact

Generational impact is found throughout Scripture. The famous passage in which Joshua declares that he and his house will serve the Lord

appears in Joshua 24, just before his death. Verse 31 of the same chapter shows the next generation who outlived Joshua and knew about God's
works among the nation of Israel. Only a few pages ahead in the Bible,
Judges 2:10 declares the spiritually fatal phrase: There arose a third generation that had no clue who God was or what He had done.

There are other examples of generational influence such as Abraham,
Isaac, and Jacob, where Abraham modeled a lie for Isaac until Abraham's
grandson Jacob is known for his deceptive ways. David fell for Bathsheba,
Solomon fell for many, and then Rehoboam split the kingdom in a wicked
fashion. From the first generation to the third, each had a different view of
God; commitment diminished with each generation.

Generational Connections

The *Shema* of Deuteronomy 6 is named so from the Hebrew word for
summons—"Hear, O Israel," or "Come listen to the Word of God." The
commands were both propositional in that they affirmed who God is and
personal in how each generation was to be committed to Him (Wright,
1996). Dr. Elmer Towns was speaking at a conference and revealed how
teachers throughout our lives were knowledgeable, but what made one
or two of them most memorable were the relationship connections that
inspired us to want to learn (Towns, 2004). This demonstrates what both
Deuteronomy and Ephesians teach about the way instruction and influence comes from close relationships, those people who help connect the
biblical lessons with everyday life.

Throughout Scripture, God the Father consistently refers to believers as His children. You cannot limit Deuteronomy 6 to a cultural setting
found only among the Israelites and only in the Old Testament. The model
of the family shows up everywhere in Scripture both Old and New Testaments. God calls us His children, He is the Father, the church is the bride
of Christ, and He adopted us into His family. Relationships become the
structure upon which instruction, discipleship, and growth can occur. Our
Father follows the same admonition as He seeks a close relationship with
His children whom He does not agitate or anger but seeks to rescue and
redeem. Without a relationship, one limits potential influence and teach-

ing. Each of the three Synoptic Gospels quote Jesus quoting the *Shema*, but Mark uses the word *ek* (the Greek preposition "with") reading it as "with all your heart," which suggests we should pursue God with our entire being, with our heart, soul, mind, and strength (Merrill, 1994). One can find generational discipleship addressed by numerous writers throughout the Bible, and more so as part of Christ's way to engage life. Even Christ reminded the disciples of the value of allowing time with the children in the midst of the busy ministry day.

When parents make a powerful connection teaching their kids a biblical worldview, then the kids can stand firm without their parents. Sounds a lot like Daniel, Shadrach, Meshach, and Abednego, who cheered for the God of their parents even when living in a foreign land. This describes the power of generational discipleship.

Paul connected the reputation of the teacher to the validity of what is taught in 2 Timothy 3:14-17. This key passage teaches inspiration, but pay close attention to the surrounding verses as well. Paul told Timothy how, from early childhood, he had been well instructed and prepared to represent the teachings of Scripture. Paul even pointed Timothy to the godly genealogy of his mom and grandmother who shaped his early life. I detest reading the genealogies. Reading genealogies in Scripture may not be the most enjoyable devotional reading but genealogies show trends, trajectories, and outliers. People's inclusion in a genealogy shows the power of generational affects and effects. God uses people to influence culture and to create lasting cultural change.

Eating Up the Denominator

If parents have such a great amount of influence, why does the numerator still show only "1," and what can the church do to change it? The logical question is, "If only one hour is spent in discipleship, what is eating up the remaining 168 hours?"

Of course, sleep consumes a big portion of this number. Arguably, most kids do not get eight hours a night, but one can assume they get seven, and that takes forty-nine hours. School absorbs another seven hours a day, taking thirty-five more hours, or five days. So after eighty-four hours for sleep and school, that leaves half the week, or another eighty-four hours—the same ones to which God referred in Deuteronomy 6. That is time spent getting up, commuting, eating, and talking. These opportune times are easy to miss in the busy-ness of the day or by absorbing some form of media.

Let us examine how media captures time and eats the denominator. Phones, for example, captivate in ways they never have before. The iPhones are so convenient. How did pastors accomplish everything back in the days before computers? Mobile technology can have some positive spiritual benefits. One in four adults have increased in time spent reading the Bible due to downloading an app (Barna, 2014a). Mobile devices provide some impressive Bible apps and ways to interact for quiet time. Technology simplifies the world and provides efficiency, but also enslaves at times both in work and socially dominated habits.

Television absorbs large blocks of time. Each week, kids watch enough hours of TV to equal the hours of a full-time job, reported a 2013 Time Magazine study. The same study also revealed that the average child spends about thirty-five hours per week watching TV and another ten hours on a gaming system (Rothman, 2013). An older study showed that ninety-nine percent of Americans owned at least one television, and the average amount of time a TV was on in the home is six hours and forty-seven minutes (Herr, 2007). The passage of time has revealed an increased use of electronics and the use of rectangles, televisions, smartphones, gaming systems, tablets, computer screens, and other similar devices.

Sixty-six percent of families eat dinner while watching TV, a California State University of Northridge (CSUN) study showed (Herr, 2007). Other studies reveal a close link between the family dinner table and outcomes in a child's life. The CSUN study also reported *meaningful conversation* between parents and kids each week averaged only three and a half minutes, (Herr, 2007) far worse than the 1/168 fraction. The parenting number has to grow. Who gets to shape the worldview of the kids in church: their parents or the Kardashians? Because of the powerful impact of multiple hours in front of the TV, it truly is hard for parents to keep up.

All this means that whether in the form of tablets, phones, television, gaming systems, or other items, rectangles consume one's—and especially one's kids'—world. How many times does a person or persons stand or sit in a group, but are not a true part of it because of their interaction with some electronic rectangle?

Fascination with mobile devices has created connected isolation. Half of all millennials admit to allowing personal electronics to separate them from other people, and thirty-five percent (just over one in three) of all adults admit the same thing. Worse, only twenty-one percent of these hyperlinked adults set aside any time to connect with God (Barna, 2014b). The typical response? "I don't have time." In truth, time is the true equalizer, because everyone has the same 168 hours.

The technology-based rectangles in society can provide tremendous value, but should not control. Food is necessary, but in moderate proportions. In the same way a scale helps monitor the results of food choices, perhaps a scale is necessary to weigh electronic usage and keep usage within a healthy range. Church leaders must make it their mission to help parents change that flawed fraction.

Raising the Numerator

Parents can change it. It is not totally fair to suggest that if the church has one hour, then the parents or home have all of the other 167, but they do have enough hours equivalent to a part-time job and that becomes their full-time job! Both dads and moms can look for more ways to interact with their kids than just sharing space in a room while connected to one or more rectangles.

The church can help connect with their kids in meaningful ways. Because parents already look to the church as experts, the church can teach parents to become a vital part of ministry. The only way parents can connect with their kids on spiritual matters is to connect on general topics throughout the week. There is a powerful message parents give to kids when they put down their phones, turn off the TV, and talk to their family or connect by playing a board game. Parents can help children with homework or sit nearby and read as the child does homework. What high school student enjoys doing algebra while Dad or Mom watches TV, and what younger child loves reviewing spelling words while Dad and Mom enjoy a movie together?

Parents may not be able to help with calculus, but they can read the math text with their child or show support by sitting nearby reading another book. If the student plays an instrument, teach parents to share their practice time by listening or again reading while they practice. Parents can also assist with drills on any sport in which their child is involved—they do not have to be experts at the sport, but they need to be in there trying.

When adding fractions, the denominator is simplified by making them the same and then adding the numerators together. If the church gets only one hour of spiritual influence each week, what number do parents get to shape their own kids' spiritual growth? Add the two numbers and grow the spiritual influence. What is interesting is how this strengthens parents as much as it does the kids.

Church leaders can show parents how to connect. This will reverse the way they think, because the typical parents bring their kids to church to be taught Scripture. They have been conditioned to do this in sports, education, and music—take them to the experts, who will teach their kids while Dad and Mom cheer from the sidelines. But what they do not realize is that their kids would greatly benefit if Dad or Mom took on a portion of that role themselves. It is not that parents do not want to be involved; they just do not know how or do not feel capable of helping. This is where church leaders should shift some attention away from the children, teens, and preschoolers and toward the parents of those same age groups. By providing more opportunities for parents to influence the kids, church leaders can help increase the numerator of influence.

No, parents do not get all of the other 167 hours of our original fraction, but they do have influence during key times like commutes, meals, and evenings at home. Since parents are the major shapers of character, values, and behavior, the church should recruit parents to reinforce the lessons from church. Parents cannot pass the kids' spiritual development off to the church alone. Instead, the church can help parents learn to pray with their kids, find scriptural answers for everyday life, use tools to reinforce the church's small group lessons, and discuss the pastor's message. Parents need to learn how to manage the rectangles, increase conversations, and invest in teachable moments. Something to remember: kids interpret the world through their parents' cues—the church helps the parents act and react for their kid's correct interpretation. This describes the power of generational discipleship. Today, it starts at church and continues in the home. One day, it could begin at home and overflow into the church. Parents are your ministry multipliers!

Deuteronomy 6 knows no time limit, no cultural boundary, and no geographical preference. Generational discipleship passages show the value of the church equipping people, making marriages stronger, and helping parents spiritually coach and guide their kids. When all of the ministries of the church find ways to strengthen parents to coach their kids, every generation wins and becomes a true disciple of Christ. Generational discipleship from both the church and home reflects God's original plan and it still works today.

References

Barna, G. (2014a). *The state of the Bible: 6 trends for 2014*. Retrieved from Ventura, CA: https://www.barna.org/barna-update/culture/664-the-state-of-the-bible-6-trends-for-2014 - .VfA6eGRVhBf

Barna, G. (2014b). *Three digital life trends for 2014*. Retrieved from Ventura, CA: https://www.barna.org/index.php?option=com_content&view=article&id=657:three-digital-life-trends-for-2014&catid=13:culture&Itemid=306 - .VfBEemRVhBd

Christensen, D. L. (2001). *Deuteronomy 1:1-21:9, revised* (2nd ed.). Nashville, TN: Thomas Nelson.

Colson, C. W., & Pearcey, N. (1999). *How now shall we live?* Wheaton, IL: Tyndale House.

Herr, N. (2007). Television & health. Retrieved from http://www.csun.edu/science/health/docs/tv&health.html - influence

Hunter, J. D. (2010). *To change the world: The irony, tragedy, and possibility of Christianity in the late modern world*. New York, NY: Oxford University Press.

Lincoln, A. T. (1990). *Ephesians*. Dallas, TX: Word Books.

Mangum, D. (2014). *Lexham theological wordbook*. Bellingham, WA: Lexham Press. Retrieved from Logos Bible software

Merrill, E. H. (1994). *The new American commentary: Deuteronomy* (Vol. 4). Nashville, TN: B. & H.

Rothman, L. (2013). FYI, Parents: Your kids watch a full-time job's worth of TV each week. Retrieved from http://entertainment.time.com/2013/11/20/fyi-parents-your-kids-watch-a-full-time-jobs-worth-of-tv-each-week/

Towns, E. (2004). *The influence of a teacher.* Paper presented at the East Coast Mid-Atlantic Christian Educators Association, New Bern, NC.

VanderKam, J. C. (1994). *The Dead Sea scrolls today.* Grand Rapids, MI: Eerdmans.

Wolters, A. M. (2005). *Creation regained: Biblical basics for a reformational worldview* (2nd ed.). Grand Rapids, MI: Eerdmans.

Woods, E. J. (2011). *Deuteronomy: An introduction and commentary.* Downers Grove, IL: IVP Academic.

Wright, C. J. H. (1996). *Deuteronomy.* Peabody, MA: Hendrickson Publishers.

Author Biography

Ron Hunter Jr. is the Executive Director, President, and CEO of Randall House Publications, and co-founder of the D6 Conference.

Ron has authored or helped author three books, *The DNA of D6: Building Blocks of Generational Discipleship, Youth Ministry in the 21st Century – 5 Views,* and *Toy Box Leadership*. He holds a BA from Welch College, an MPA from the University of Colorado, and is currently a Ph.D. candidate at Dallas Baptist University. Ron Hunter Jr. is the CEO of Randall House, and he is the Director of the D6 Conference, but his favorite titles are Husband and Father.

The Relationship Between the Duties of Fatherhood From a Biblical Worldview With Modern-Day Christian Fatherhood

Brian S. McKinney

Over the last five decades, various questions have been raised examining the unique role that fathers play in the healthy development of a child. Debates over the necessity of a father have strengthened the controversy surrounding the idea of what the nuclear family should consist in order to give children the best opportunity for success in social skills, psychological development, education, and careers. On one side of the argument, conservative scholars argue for the traditional two-parent home with both genders represented because there are certain roles to be carried out, which only a mother can perform and certain roles only a father can perform in the development of the child. On the other side of the argument, liberal scholars argue the roles of the father can be divided up amongst the mother, grandparents, aunts, uncles, friends, teachers, and significant partners. Lisa Dodson, a feminist scholar, believes women evolve into a stronger, more independent parent with resiliency compensating for the lack of the father (Daniels, ed., 1998, p. 6); however, very little research can be found to back the liberal argument comparing successful single-parenting or same-sex, two-parent homes versus the traditional, nuclear two-gender parent team.

Upon beginning the research for the effect of children's outcomes from fatherless homes, the researcher discovered a plethora of material consisting of studies performed over the last two decades. With the current technology, one can use a search engine and find hundreds of articles referencing studies on fatherhood and fatherless homes. While considering a content analysis of the literature on the effect of fatherless homes, it became clear what was missing in the research was the element of fathering from a biblical worldview.

The book that started the interest and drive for the research and is considered a landmark book in the area of fatherless homes, Fatherless America: Confronting our Most Urgent Social Problem, revealed a rational argument for the need to study the importance of a father in a child's life for the sake of future generations and society. David Blankenhorn, founder and president of the Institute of American Values and author of this most influential work on fatherless homes, summarizes the diminishment of American fatherhood by stating the following four traditional characteristics of fatherhood are becoming lost in society: father as irreplaceable caregiver, moral educator, head of family, and family breadwinner (Blankenhorn, 1995, p. 16). Children without fathers do not fare well in the world of academia, or in society, due to their upbringing without the consistent father-figure available in the home. In addition, the connection of social pathologies with fatherless homes is so strong that some researchers have concluded the likelihood of children's involvement in crime is determined by the extent of the involvement of both parents in their children's lives, rather than income or race (Baskerville, 2004, p. 3).

Another seminal work, The Role of the Father in Child Development, has been revised and updated five times over the past two decades with more and more research confirming the role of a father as well as the effect a father has on a child. Michael Lamb, head of the Social and Emotional Development section at the National Institute of Child Health and Human Development in Bethesda, Maryland, and author of this book, explains the roles of fatherhood from a secular perspective: companion, care provider, protector, model, moral guide, teacher, and breadwinner (2004, p. 3).

David Popenoe, author of Families without Fathers, summarizes how feminists and liberals have concluded that the roles of fathers are not essential by taking the common roles of fatherhood and showing how those roles can be substituted amongst many people, in addition to the constant negativity toward fathers. In his book, he espouses four arguments frequently used in the debate against fathers:

- Women no longer need monetary provisions because of the independent labor market for women, as well as government subsidized programs and welfare.
- Women do not need men for protection because of the availability of the police, and the protection they need is usually from their male partner.
- Males bring a patriarchal institution of dominance over mothers, and are selfish, irresponsible, and psychologically untrustworthy.
- In the midst of crisis, men leave their wives and children either through psychological withdrawal or desertion (2009, p. 9).

The researcher acknowledges in some cases, the arguments against having a father involved in a child's life may indeed be true; however, without research and data, there cannot be definite conclusions to the authenticity of the feminist arguments.

Paul Amato, researcher, family scholar, and author of many studies and articles involving marriage and families, concluded from his vast amount of research that fathers are extremely important to the welfare of their children. This is true not simply from an economic standpoint or peripheral role, but an involved, nurturing, and emotional standpoint. From his review of the literature prior to performing his 1994 study, he explains that several types of research support the notion that fathers are important. One cluster of studies examines correlations between father involvement and child outcomes. This research, reviewed by Lamb (1987), Radin and Russell (1983), and Snarey (1993), is generally supportive of the role of fathers. Father involvement and nurturance are positively associated with children's intellectual development; this is particularly true when fathers are interested in children's academic outcomes, assist with homework, and have high educational expectations for their children. In addition, father involvement and nurturance are positively associated with children's social competence, internal locus of control, and the ability to empathize (Amato, 1994, pp. 1031-1032).

The research for this article is pertinent to the traditional nuclear family structure and the 21st century church of Christ. With the multitude of published studies and government initiatives proposed since the late 20th century dealing with children coming from homes without fathers, it appears this topic will continue to be addressed as one of the leading causes associated with modern-day children's low-functioning academia and high rise of social misbehaviors. One can easily establish a relationship between father engagement and a child's academic and social behaviors from a variety of scholarly studies via the Internet and library databases, and in a large majority of the reports from various states in America and other countries around the world. The multitude of studies the researcher has come into contact with all came to the same conclusions: children from fatherless homes had more social behavioral issues, psychological issues, academic difficulties, and a higher percentage of incarcerations.

While many 20th and 21st century family scholars have attempted to define the roles of fathers based on observations and longitudinal studies, there has not been a definite list produced that can specifically define the roles of fathers from a historical and theological perspective based on God as a father to His people. Many secular psychologists lean toward the understanding that the essential development of a child is based on the nurture from a mother, thus effecting the changes in government law about divorce and the promotion of alternate definitions of family. Consequently, a revival among Christian father apologists occurred to counteract the amount of negative effects in children outcomes without fathers involved in the family.

In recent years, theologians have attempted to address the roles of fathers in order to help maintain a complementary understanding of Scripture involving fathers' and mothers' roles; however, there has been a lack of consistency in development of a definite list. Often, the roles are based on traditional Judeo-Christian history with a mixture of examples from biblical passages. By examining the Hebrew Scriptures, also recognized as the Old Testament in the Christian Bible, involving God describing Himself as a father to His people, this current research has provided a definite list of seven roles a father must effectively carry out in his involvement with his children. The places in the Old Testament where the name of Yahweh (YHWH) is associated with "Father" are listed in order from the Christian Bible: Deuteronomy 32:6; 2 Samuel 7:14-15; 1 Chronicles 17:13, 22:10, 28:6; Psalm 89:26; Isaiah 63:16, 64:8; Jeremiah 3:4, 31:9; and Malachi 1:6a. From these 11 passages of Scripture, the researcher discovered several passages were almost exact phrases in the same places; however, a definite list of six roles of fathers was discovered based on God the Father as the example: merciful disciplinarian, protector of children, provider, trusting friend, demonstrator of leadership, and instructor of education, trade, faith, morality, and respect.

From each of these roles, one should be able to conceptually understand that God the Father loved and cared for His children without the specific words mentioned. The researcher felt it was important to examine the New Testament to discover if any other roles of God the Father could be added to the list. With 170 references of God the Father, many of the above-mentioned roles were reinforced. The most important role of a father was confirmed in two very familiar passages: John 3:16 and Romans 5:8. John 3:16 reads, "For God so loved the world that He gave His only begotten Son, that whoever believes in Him shall not perish, but have eternal life" (New American Standard Bible, NASB). Romans 5:8 states, "But God demonstrates His own love toward us, in that while we were yet sinners, Christ died for us" (NASB). Understanding God the Father has demonstrated His love for His children sacrificially, should help the 21st century father recognize another featured role in fatherhood is to love his children.

Using these seven roles of fatherhood as the main roles, one can adapt each category to further establish lists of ways fathers can demonstrate these seven essential roles of fatherhood based on God the Father as the primary example of how to be a father. The survey for Christian fathers assessed their understanding of the seven essential roles portrayed by God the Father: protecting, providing, disciplining, leading, teaching, being a friend, and loving His children. Through the use of a survey instrument called the Roles of Christian Fathers Questionnaire, the researcher gained insights into what modern day fathers believe to be the most important roles, as well as the least important roles, and also discovered some of the key reasons why the fathers (N=241) who participated in the study believe they are or are not proficient in the seven essential roles of fatherhood.

Using a Likert scale of 1-7, each number represented had a specific meaning (1 meaning "very poor," 2 meaning "poor," 3 meaning "not adequate," 4 meaning "neutral," 5 meaning "adequate," 6 meaning "good," and 7 meaning "excellent"). The answers are based on fathers either from a Catholic or Protestant background reporting their involvement with their children in the last 12 months. From the Likert scale scoring, an average score of one to three would be considered "below proficient" in fathering, a score of four would be "average," and a score of five to seven would be "proficient" in fathering. The top scoring categories according to the fathers were: providing for their children's basic needs ($\mu = 6.79$, $\sigma = 0.53$), financial support ($\mu = 6.77$, $\sigma = 0.62$), and telling their child they love them ($\mu = 6.56$, $\sigma = 0.80$). The areas where fathers indicate they need to improve based on a lower score in the categories surveyed include: reading to their child ($\mu = 4.51$, $\sigma = 1.42$), effectiveness in teaching their child a trade ($\mu = 4.96$, $\sigma = 1.20$), and encouraging their children to do chores ($\mu = 5.26$, $\sigma = 1.17$). With the lowest score being reading, one might perceive that reading to their children is to be done in the early years of childhood and not throughout adolescence. Thinking biblically, a father is responsible for reading and teaching the Scriptures to his children throughout their time being with them.

In looking at the seven essential roles of fatherhood based on God the Father's example, providing for the child again was positioned as the highest categorical average ($\mu = 6.48$, $\sigma = 0.77$) while being a friend to their child was scored as the lowest ($\mu = 5.46$, $\sigma = 1.07$). Ranking in order of how the seven essential categories were scored from highest to lowest, the fathers in this survey determined the order to be: providing, protecting, loving/nurturing, instruction, leading, discipline, and being a friend.

Table 1

Descriptive Statistics for Roles of Christian Fathers Questionnaire (ROCFQ)

Questions	M	SD
Attending events where child participated	6.24	0.99
Encouraging your child to read	5.47	1.23
Providing the basic needs	6.79	0.53
Praising child for doing the right thing	6.13	0.79
Giving support to mother and encouraging her	5.48	1.25
Being involved in routine of caregiving	6.11	1.03
Letting child know their mother is important	5.63	1.27
Praising child for doing something well	6.21	0.85
Encouraging your child to succeed in school	6.32	0.85
Being a friend or pal to your child	5.46	1.04
Accepting responsibility for financial support	6.77	0.62
Encouraging your child to do their homework	6.06	0.92
Telling your child you love them	6.56	0.80
Knowing where your child is and what he/she is doing	6.40	0.91
Spending time talking with your child	5.82	0.97
Cooperating with child's mother in rearing child	6.18	0.98
Reading to your child	4.51	1.42
Teaching your child to obey and follow rules	6.21	0.68
Encouraging child in higher education	6.05	1.23
Disciplining your child	5.81	0.77
Helping child with homework	5.27	1.16
Helping child plan their future (education/occupation)	5.51	1.19
Encouraging child to develop talents	6.03	0.93
Spending time with child doing what they like to do	5.63	1.10
Encouraging your child to do chores	5.26	1.17
Setting rules and limits for behavior of child	5.89	0.76
Effectiveness in loving and nurturing child	6.15	0.78
Effectiveness in disciplining child	5.57	0.84
Effectiveness in protecting child	6.28	0.85
Effectiveness in providing for child	6.48	0.77
Effectiveness in being a friend to child	5.43	1.07
Effectiveness in leading by example for the child	5.72	0.99
Effectiveness in instructing child in academic subjects	5.53	1.02
Effectiveness in instructing child in faith	5.68	1.13
Effectiveness in instructing child in morality	6.09	0.77
Effectiveness in instructing child to respect others	6.15	0.87
Effectiveness in instructing child in a trade	4.96	1.20
Overall effectiveness in instructing child	5.80	0.73

For this study, each of the seven essential roles had questions placed at the end of the ROCFQ survey to allow for open-ended responses by the fathers. In each of the questions asking for the fathers to rate themselves on the seven essential roles of being a father, the respondents presented a rationale for why they scored themselves proficient or deficient in each category resulting in qualitative data. Each of the essential roles of fathers will have some of these sample answers from the fathers as well as any significant statistical information reported in tables or provided throughout the text.

For the quantitative data, the researcher chose to identify the individual questions from the original IFI as independent variables while identifying the ratings of the seven questions dealing specifically with the essential roles as the dependent variables for the statistical tests being conducted. The purpose was to investigate if the answers that the fathers provided for the open-ended questions showed a correlation with the individual questions that can be placed under each of the seven roles.

Provide

Starting with the first category scoring the highest among the seven, here are some key words provided by the fathers explaining why they believed they were above proficient: feed them, cloth them, and give them shelter; send them to a private Christian school; provisions for financial, emotional, and physical needs; material needs beyond basic needs; safe environment; provisions for talents and interests; have life insurance and financial accounts set up in advance should something happen to the parents; a plan for college; and earthly and spiritual needs met.

Interesting to note, of the 201 respondents in the proficient category of providing for their children, only 21 mentioned meeting the spiritual needs of their children (10.4%). Granted, some of the responses were all-inclusive stating all their needs are met; however, one cannot assume the provision of spiritual needs being met. This is an area of great concern for the 21st century churches of Christ moving forward, as parents appear to be under the assumption that all spiritual needs can be met by sending their children to church or a Christian school without taking the time necessary to make sure their children have a God-ward orientation of living through prayer, Bible reading and study, as well as discipleship. In addition, combing the lack of provision of spiritual needs with the lowest ranked survey question by the responses of the fathers in the survey, and one can see reading the Bible is not a priority in many homes despite the Scriptures pointing to the necessity of fathers to read God's Word to their children (Deuteronomy 6:7-9).

While an overall majority of the fathers scored themselves very high in this category, some of the fathers in the evaluation of their own efforts in providing for their children responded with below proficient. Some of the reasons why they scored themselves lower include: not providing spiritually for them, not enough time in the day to meet all of the children's needs, not having premium healthcare, not able to provide them a Christian education, not having a strong plan financially, and not having enough time to provide for all of their needs. Interesting to note for the eight comments on the negative side of provisions, three were pointed at the lack of provision for their children's spiritual needs.

For the statistical portion of the category of fathers providing for their children, the first statistical test completed was a correlation test to determine the measure of strength between the three independent variables and the dependent variable. The R-value for the correlation was 0.615, meaning a strong, positive linear correlation between the variables.

In Table 2, a one-way between subjects ANOVA was conducted to compare the effect of three constant variables (financial support, involvement in the regular routine of taking care of the children, and taking care of children's basic needs) on the effectiveness of fathers providing for their children. There was a significant effect of the independent variables on the dependent variable at the $p < 0.05$ level for the two conditions [$F (3, 236) = 47.876$, $p = 0.000$]. Taken together, these results suggest that the three constant variables mentioned above do have a relationship on the ratings that the fathers had of themselves in providing for their children.

Table 2

ANOVA Regression for Providing

	Sum of Squares	df	Mean Square	F	p
Regression	52.928	3	17.643	47.876	0.000
Residual	86.968	236	0.369		
Total	139.896	239			

p < 0.001

Looking at Table 3, the coefficient values for each independent variable were calculated against the dependent variable of the ratings the respondent fathers gave themselves in the area of providing for their children.

Table 3

Coefficient Values for Each Independent Variable

	Unstandardized Coefficients		Standardized Coefficients		
	B	SE B	Beta	t	p
Constant	-0.580	0.593	-0.978	0.329	
Rate yourself in accepting financial responsibility for children	0.547	0.082	0.373	6.647	0.000
Rate yourself in being involved in the regular routine of child care	0.083	0.039	0.111	2.128	0.034
Rate yourself on taking care of your children's basic needs	0.418	0.070	0.334	6.010	0.000

p < 0.05.

Protect

The second highest ranked category involved protecting their children. While the survey did not have as many questions pointed toward this specific category as the other essential roles of fatherhood did, the open-ended answers helped fill in some of the areas needing to be addressed within this essential role of fathers in future studies of fatherhood. To investigate the list of questions, the reader may use the actual survey found in the shortened form of the questions found in Table 2 involving the descriptive statistics of each of the questions on the ROCFQ. Some of the 209 father responses indicating proficient in this study include: watching out who they hang with, keeping them from inappropriate TV shows and websites, monitoring and limiting their influences, and providing for home security and a safe home.

Similarly to the category of providing, the area of protecting had very few comments on the deficient side. Of the seven respondents, items the area of scoring deficient include: lack of protecting children from poor eating habits, not enough supervision for outside play, not preventing child from being bullied at school, not able to protect them from drugs and other worldly items, not enough teaching about safety (what to look out for, the "what ifs"), and not enough time to protect the children from what the world can offer.

For the statistical portion of this category involving fathers protecting their children, it was discovered this was the one area where improvement should have been made in adding more questions to the survey. Only two questions in the ROCFQ were asked: rate yourself in knowing where your children go and what they do with their friends (independent variable), and rate yourself in protecting your children (dependent variable). Statistical information reported here is based simply on one independent variable and the dependent variable. A correlation test was conducted and yielded a R-value of 0.294 indicating a weak correlation between the responses on the two questions.

A one-way between subjects ANOVA was conducted to compare the effect of the constant variable (knowing where your children go and what they do with their friends) on the effectiveness of fathers protecting their children. There was a significant effect of the independent variable on the dependent variable at the $p < 0.05$ level for the two conditions [$F_{(1, 238)} = 22.447$, $p = 0.000$]. This result suggests the constant variable mentioned above does have a relationship on fathers perceptions of themselves in protecting their children.

Table 4

ANOVA Regression (Protect)

	Sum of Squares	df	Mean Square	F	p
Regression	14.849	1	14.849	22.447	0.000
Residual	157.446	238	0.662		
Total	172.296	239			

$p < 0.001$.

Looking at Table 5, the coefficient values for each independent variable were calculated against the dependent variable of the ratings the fathers gave themselves in the area of protecting their children.

Table 5

Coefficient Values for Each Independent Variable (Protect)

	Unstandardized Coefficients		Standardized Coefficients		
	B	SE B	Beta	t	p
Constant	4.516	0.376		12.011	0.000
Rate yourself in knowing where your children go and who they are with	0.275	0.058	0.294	4.738	0.000

$p < 0.001$.

Love

The third highest ranked category according to the survey results of the seven essential roles of fatherhood is the roles of loving and nurturing children. Of the 212 father respondents, many of the responses dealt with physical affection, continual encouragement, and verbally expressing how much they love their children, demonstrating their love through spending quality time with the children, praising and disciplining, and doing activities their children enjoy with them. Interesting to note, 16 respondents mentioned God or Jesus in their comments about love. 1 John 4:8 teaches readers that God is love and because of this essential truth to a Christian father, teaching about God's love for their children is a vital component of a child's upbringing as many children will associate their earthly father with the Heavenly Father.

In the comments under the category of feeling deficient as a father in the area of loving their children, there were only six respondents. The six comments were: overreacting to their children in a negative way when they should discipline with love, being angry too often to love, too hard on the children, not enough time, too tired and too busy to demonstrate love for their children, and everyone has room for growth according to the standards of the Bible. Given the Bible indicates two words throughout the Greek New Testament using the word love, it can be very easy to understand how someone would say they are deficient in the area of love depending on which way they define love. The two words for love in the Greek New Testament are αγαπαω, meaning sacrificial love, the highest form of love, a total commitment kind of love, and φιλεω, meaning simply love for a friend or brotherly love (Aland et al., 2001, p. 97). The passage of John 21:15-17 demonstrates the differences in these words beautifully as the resurrected Jesus Christ is restoring Peter after the latter had made claims that he would never deny Jesus and then indeed he did deny the Christ on three occasions. In the passage, Jesus asks Peter if he loves Him sacrificially on the first two occasions and Peter cannot respond with the same higher form of sacrificial love (αγαπαω), but instead replies with the lower form of love (φιλεω) that being the love for a friend. On the final occasion, Jesus asks if Peter did indeed love Him as a friend. As recorded in the book of John, chapter 18, Peter previously was humbled when the Lord Jesus predicted Peter would deny being a follower of Jesus three times when asked by people in the crowds during the crucifixion of the Messiah; therefore, Jesus gave him three opportunities to be restored.

For the statistical portion of the category of fathers loving their children, the first statistical test completed was a correlation test to determine the measure of strength between the four independent variables and the dependent variable. The R-value for the correlation was 0.643, meaning a strong, positive linear correlation between the variables.

In Table 6, a one-way between subjects ANOVA was conducted to compare the effect of four constant variables (spending time doing things your children like to do, telling your children you love them, praising your children for being good or doing the right thing, and praising your children for doing something well) on the effectiveness of fathers loving their children. There was a significant effect of the independent variables on the dependent variable at the $p < 0.05$ level for the two conditions [$F(4, 235) = 41.543$, $p = 0.000$]. Taken together, these results suggest the four constant variables mentioned above do have a relationship on fathers rating of themselves in loving their children.

Table 6

ANOVA Regression for Love

	Sum of Squares	df	Mean Square	F	p
Regression	60.291	4	15.073	41.543	0.000
Residual	85.626	236	0.363		
Total	145.917	240			

p < 0.001.

Looking at Table 7, the coefficient values for each independent variable were calculated against the dependent variable of the fathers rating of themselves in the area of loving their children.

Table 7

Coefficient Values for Each Independent Variable (Love)

	Unstandardized Coefficients		Standardized Coefficients		
	B	SE B	Beta	t	p
Constant	1.539	0.386		3.989	0.000
Rate yourself in praising your children for being good	0.186	0.064	0.188	2.929	0.004*
Rate yourself in praising your children for doing something well	-0.015	0.060	-0.016	-0.244	0.807
Rate yourself on telling them you love them	0.342	0.056	0.350	6.097	0.000*
Rate yourself in spending time with your children doing things they like	0.233	0.038	0.327	6.105	0.000*

*p < 0.05.

Teach

The fourth highest ranked category according to the father respondents was the area of teaching. Inside the area of teaching or instructing, there were questions dealing with academic instruction, teaching their children a trade, instructing on morality, and instructing on respect. There were 160 open-ended responses dealing with this category and of these, 45 of the comments were directly focused on reading and teaching from the Bible. While 28 percent of these respondents mentioned instruction of faith through devotionals, daily Bible reading with children, and teaching of morality and respect based on God's word, there were many comments directed at how they sent their children to a private Christian school and also taking them to church. The latter two comments are certainly admirable, it should be noted that the responsibility of teaching children about Jesus and how to live based on God's Word falls directly on the fathers and not contracted out to children's and youth pastors or Christian educators (Deutetonomy 6:4-9; Isaiah 38:19). Other common answers included: helping their children with their homework, monitoring their grades and progress, encouraging them in their interests for vocation after school, the children's mother handles the academics, and demonstrating moral living and respecting others.

In the comments under the category of feeling deficient as a father in the area of instructing their children, the fathers wrote about not having devotional time with their children, nobody is perfect, teaching respect is a work in progress, working to be a better example for the children, and mediocre in helping the children develop their faith. Helping fathers develop their children's faith is an area where male mentoring in the churches as well as discipleship classes must be offered to help the 21st century dads and families. While the times have changed and interests in societies across the globe has changed, God's Word has not and the Bible is specific about the role of the father in instruction.

For the statistical portion of the category of fathers instructing their children, it became necessary to use stepwise regression as there were several predicator variables involved determining if the relationship between the nine independent predictor variables and the dependent variable of the fathers rating their effectiveness in teaching their children. The multiple R-value for the correlation was 0.622, meaning a strong, positive linear correlation between the variables.

In Table 8, a one-way between subjects ANOVA was conducted to compare the effect of four constant variables (helping with homework, encouraging children to succeed in school, encouraging children to read, and developing their talents) on the effectiveness of fathers teaching their children. There was a significant effect of the independent variables on the dependent variable at the $p < 0.05$ level for the two conditions [$F(4, 229) = 23.611$, $p = 0.000$]. Taken together, these results suggest that the four constant variables mentioned above do have a relationship on fathers rating of themselves in teaching their children.

Table 8

ANOVA Model 4 Regression for Teaching

	Sum of Squares	df	Mean Square	F	p
Regression	94.446	4	23.611	36.100	0.000
Residual	149.781	229	0.654		
Total	244.227	239			

$p < 0.001$.

Looking at Table 9, the coefficient values for each independent variable were calculated against the dependent variable of the fathers rating themselves in the area of teaching their children.

Table 9

Coefficient Values for Each Independent Variable

	Unstandardized Coefficients		Standardized Coefficients		
	B	SE B	Beta	t	p
Constant	0.263	0.483	0.545	0.586	
Rate yourself in helping children with homework	0.299	0.050	0.338	5.978	0.000
Rate yourself on encouraging your children to succeed in school	0.322	0.069	0.263	4.672	0.000
Rate yourself on encouraging your children to read	0.131	0.046	0.157	2.840	0.005
Rate yourself in encouraging your children to develop their talents	0.154	0.062	0.140	2.497	0.013

$p < 0.05$.

Lead

The fifth highest ranked category according to the father respondents was the area of leading children. Of the 182 open-ended responses in the area of proficiency as a father in this category, overwhelmingly the same phrases came up including "lead by example," "living what you say," and "talk the talk, walk the walk." The respondents also included many other noteworthy items such as showing leadership by admitting mistakes and correcting them by asking forgiveness, demonstrating how to serve others, and mentioning demonstrating how to walk in faith with their children. The latter item about demonstrating leadership through modeling a Christian walk and lifestyle was mentioned in 62 responses (34%).

In the area of being deficient in leadership for their children, the fathers who responded were very open in their responses. While there were only 15 responses, a wide range of items appear as to why 21st century fathers may believe they are not proficient in leading their children. Some of the responses include: raise voice in anger too often, drinking, swearing, laziness, can be better in leading spiritually, not perfect, can do much better, lose my temper, inappropriate actions, leading by bad example, not demonstrating Christ, not consistent in demonstrating Christ, too many negative actions demonstrated, thought I was leading correctly but my child went astray, and my wife is the leader in our home. Of all the categories, with the candid answers given, the church can help in this category through discipleship classes and through encouraging male mentors to help young fathers become better fathers.

For the statistical portion of the category for fathers leading their children, the first statistical test completed was a correlation test to determine the measure of strength between the four independent variables and the dependent variable. The R-value for the correlation was 0.470, meaning a moderate, positive linear correlation between the variables.

In Table 10, a one-way between subjects ANOVA was conducted to compare the effect of four constant variables (encouraging children to do their chores, letting your children know their mother is important, cooperating with the mother in rearing children, and giving mother encouragement and emotional support) on the effectiveness of fathers leading their children. There was a significant effect of the independent variables on the dependent variable at the $p < 0.05$ level for the two conditions [$F(4, 235) = 16.613$, $p = 0.000$]. The results suggest the four constant variables mentioned above do have a relationship on fathers rating of themselves in leading their children.

Table 10

ANOVA Regression for Leading

	Sum of Squares	df	Mean Square	F	p
Regression	51.648	4	12.912	16.613	0.000
Residual	182.647	235	0.777		
Total	234.296	239			

$p < 0.001$.

Looking at Table 11, the coefficient values for each independent variable were calculated against the dependent variable of the fathers rating themselves in the area of leading their children.

Table 11

Coefficient Values for Each Independent Variable (Lead)

	Unstandardized Coefficients		Standardized Coefficients		
	B	SE B	Beta	t	p
Constant	2.943	0.397		7.403	0.000
Rate yourself in encouraging and emotionally supporting mother	0.179	0.065	0.226	2.747	0.006*
Rate yourself in letting your children know their mom is important	0.055	0.062	0.070	0.881	0.379
Rate yourself in cooperating with the mother	0.050	0.082	0.049	0.609	0.543
Rate yourself in encouraging the children to do their chores	0.224	0.052	0.265	4.331	0.000*

*$p < 0.05$.

Discipline

Ranking number six in the list of essential roles of fatherhood is the area of discipline according to the respondent fathers in this survey. In the area of being proficient as fathers, there were 203 respondents to the open-ended portion of the survey. Many of the responses include: boundaries being set, consistency is the key, consequences matching the severity of the mistake, different methods for punishing (spanking, taking items away, grounding), tiered levels of punishment (similar to the school's discipline policy), firm but fair, and disciplining with love. Hebrews 12:4-11 speak to the believer to help understand that if the earthly father is to discipline for penalties, that the Heavenly Father will also do the same as a way of leading the believer back to Him. Of these 203 responses, only four responses mentioned God or Jesus, while three others used fathering tips from Tedd Tripp, author of Shepherding Your Child's Heart, and Josh McDowell's The Father Connection.

In the area of being deficient in discipline for children, only five fathers responded. The responses dealt with being too harsh, not hard enough, being angry when punishing, child continues in unacceptable behavior, and not enough consistency. Throughout the responses both in the proficient or deficient category, communication after the penalty being assessed was an area that needed more consistency as well.

For the statistical portion of the category discipline, it became necessary to use stepwise regression as there were several predicator variables involved determining if the relationship between the six independent predictor variables and the dependent variable of the fathers rating their effectiveness in disciplining their children. The multiple R-value for the correlation was 0.650, meaning a strong, positive linear correlation between the variables.

In Table 12, a one-way between subjects ANOVA was conducted to compare the effect of two constant variables (setting rules and limits on behavior; rating on disciplining children) on the effectiveness of fathers disciplining their children. There was a significant effect of the independent variables on the dependent variable at the $p < 0.05$ level for the two conditions [$F(2, 237) = 86.866$, $p = 0.000$]. Taken together, these results suggest that setting rules and limits for children's behavior do have a relationship on fathers rating of themselves in disciplining their children overall.

Table 12

ANOVA Model 2 Regression (Discipline)

	Sum of Squares	df	Mean Square	F	p
Regression	71.456	2	35.728	86.866	0.000
Residual	97.477	237	0.410		
Total	168.940	239			

p < 0.001.

Looking at Table 13, the coefficient values for each independent variable were calculated against the dependent variable of the fathers rating themselves in the area of disciplining their children.

Table 13

Coefficient Values for Each Independent Variable (Discipline)

	Unstandardized Coefficients		Standardized Coefficients		
	B	SE B	Beta	t	p
Constant	0.849	0.360	2.358	0.019	
Setting rules and limits for children's behavior	0.426	0.066	0.387	6.427	0.000
Rate yourself in disciplining your children	0.380	0.066	0.346	5.751	0.000

p < 0.05.

Friend

According to the respondent fathers in this study, the least significant role of the seven essential roles of a father based on God the Father's example is the area of being a friend. Of the 170 responses to the open-ended question of rating themselves in the area of being a friend, the fathers responded with many of the same answers: talking and listening to their children, spending time playing games and doing things they like (fishing, hunting, other forms of recreation, wrestling and tickling), supporting them through their school and extracurricular activities, and doing things they deem important.

The comments posted in the open-ended section of this question about this particular role of fathers occurring most often were phrased that they are parents first and friends second or that the fathers indicated they were simply the parent and never intend on being their child's friend. Comments similar to both of those in the previous sentence occurred in 34 of the 170 responses (20%). Why the fathers selected themselves as proficient in the area of being a friend is not known with the amount of negative comments appearing about being a friend. Many of those fathers added comments such as they do things that friends do with their children (talk, listen, play games) but refused to be associated as a friend or "pal" to their children. In the Bible, it is clear, God is a friend to His children (John 15:13-15; James 2:23). By His example, it is acceptable for fathers to be a parent and to be a friend at the same time.

Being the lowest ranked category of the seven essential roles of fathers, there were more comments available in the "not proficient" level of the Likert scale on the survey. Of the 16 comments written in the open-ended section of the survey, 15 of the fathers indicated similar comments to the ones listed in the above paragraph about not being a friend to their children. Phrases such as, "I do not believe you can raise a child and be their friend" or "I am their father, not their peer" were commonly stated in some form throughout the 15 comments.

For the statistical portion of the category for fathers being a friend to their children, the first statistical test completed was a correlation test to determine the measure of strength between the four independent variables and the dependent variable. The R-value for the correlation was 0.778, meaning a very strong, positive linear correlation between the variables.

In Table 14, a one-way between subjects ANOVA was conducted to compare the effect of five constant variables (attending events your children participate in, being a pal, spending time talking, encouraging your children to develop their talents, and spending time doing things with your children they like) on the effectiveness of fathers being a friend to their children. There was a significant effect of the independent variables on the dependent variable at the $p < 0.05$ level for the two conditions [F (5,

234) = 71.745, p = 0.000]. The results suggest the four constant variables mentioned above do have a relationship on fathers rating of themselves in being a friend to their children.

Table 14

ANOVA Regression (Friend)

	Sum of Squares	df	Mean Square	F	p
Regression	165.183	5	33.037	71.745	0.000
Residual	107.750	234	0.460		
Total	272.933	239			

$p < 0.001.$

Looking at Table 15, the coefficient values for each independent variable were calculated against the dependent variable of the fathers rating themselves in the area of being a friend to their children.

Table 15

Coefficient Values for Each Independent Variable (Friend)

	Unstandardized Coefficients		Standardized Coefficients		
	B	SE B	Beta	t	p
Constant	-0.493	0.435	-1.132	0.259	
Rate yourself in attending events your children participate in	0.051	0.047	0.047	1.101	0.272
Rate yourself for being a pal to your children	0.718	0.044	0.698	16.462	0.000*
Rate yourself on spending time talking with your children	0.159	0.057	0.144	2.799	0.006*
Rate yourself in encouraging your children to develop their talents	0.147	0.052	0.127	2.845	0.005*
Rate yourself on spending time doing things with your children they like	-0.023	0.050	-0.024	-0.460	0.646

$*p < 0.05.$

Statistically Significant Findings

Upon completion of the statistical tests conducted, the researcher was elated to find the amount of statistically significant items on the tests run for the seven essential roles of fathers. Each of the seven categories had a one-way ANOVA test performed comparing the effect of the constant variables on these essential roles and for each test the results showed a statistically significant level of confidence scoring with a $p < 0.001$.

In addition to the ANOVA tests, linear regression tests were also performed, and in each of the seven categories there were significant statistical findings between the independent variables and the dependent variable of the fathers rating themselves in the seven essential roles of fatherhood. Looking further into linear regression for correlation between the questions about the roles of fatherhood with the actual essential roles of fatherhood, one can see in each of the roles a majority of the independent variables showed statistically significant results to the dependent variable. These results give the reader a better understanding about the smaller details of 21st century Christian fatherhood aligning with the seven essential roles of fatherhood by the data showing a strong, positive linear correlation between the variables in five of the seven essential roles of fathers (provide, discipline, teach, love, friend), while lead still showed a moderate correlation.

Do 21st century fathers reflect the presence of the seven essential roles of fatherhood as put forth by God the Father? According to the answers provided by the 241 men who participated in the survey, the answer is unequivocally yes. Reflecting on the average score per question and in the comments for each role in the open-ended question portion of the survey, one can tell from the research that fathers believe they perform these seven roles in their children's lives. The open-ended questions did not yield much information in whether or not the fathers understood the connection between God the Father's example and the seven essential roles of fatherhood as very few times God was mentioned and never as setting an example. Because of this, it would be beneficial for churches in the 21st century to do a better job teaching who God the Father is to His children as well as the seven essential roles He teaches fathers to perform.

References

Amato, P. R. (1994). Father-child relations, mother-child relations, and off-spring psychological well-being in early adulthood. *Journal of Marriage and Family*, 56(4), 1031-1042.

Blankenhorn, D. (1995) *Fatherless America: Confronting our most urgent social problem*. New York, NY: HarperCollins.

Daniels, C., ed. (1998). *Lost fathers: The politics of fatherlessness in America*. New York, NY: St. John's Press.

Lamb, M. E., ed. (2004). *The role of the father in child development*, (4th ed.). New York, NY: Wiley.

Popenoe, D. (2009). *Families without fathers: Fathers, marriage, and children in American society*. New Brunswick, NJ: Transaction.

Author Biography

Dr. Brian S. McKinney earned an Ed.D. from Southeastern Baptist Theological Seminary and presently serves as a Principal at Mt. Juliet Christian Academy in Mt. Juliet, Tennessee.

The All-Encompassing Nature of Stewardship and Its Relevance to Christian Parenting

Sudi Gliebe

The basic etymology of the word steward (*oikonomos*) comes from two root words: *oikos*, which means house and *nomos*, which means law (McMahon, 2009). The steward is the "law over the house, and all that is associated with the house. He is given authority over the household but does not own the household" (McMahon, 2009, p.). Christian stewards accept that everything they own belongs to God (Psalm 24:1), because everything they have was given to them by God (1 Corinthians 4:7). God declares: "You are mine because I made you, and you are mine because I redeemed you" (McKay, 1974, p. 35).

McKay (1974) declares, "When one accepts the ownership of God and the stewardship of man, he becomes a partner with God" (p. 36). That partnership involves surrendering all to Christ and inviting Him to bless, guide, and use believers and their possessions for His glory. Stewardship involves not only partnership, but also responsibility. The privilege of stewardship is accompanied by a serious responsibility to follow God on His terms. Therefore the rights and benefits of Christian stewards come with a price tag (McKay, 1974).

Stewardship Is Lordship

Bible teacher David Jeremiah (2010) believes that biblical stewardship is not an aspect of Christianity; instead stewardship encompasses every area of the Christian life (Proverbs 3:5). Jeremiah (2010) often defines stewardship with one single word, Lordship. He asserts: "God is not interested in your time, your talents or your money. God is interested in you (Mt.7:13-14, 21). He wants to be the Lord of all your life" (Jeremiah, 2010, p.). The belief that Christian stewardship deals exclusively with finances is a grave misconception. Biblical stewardship must not be reduced to tithing and budgeting. On the contrary, believers must embrace the concept that "stewardship is as comprehensive as life itself" (McKay, 1974, p. 13).

McKay (1974) believes that biblical stewardship demands that believers dethrone themselves and enthrone Jesus Christ as the Supreme Lord of all. In the measure that the church embraces complete biblical stewardship, it will move away from an unbiblical emphasis on money (McKay, 1974). All-encompassing stewardship is the only kind of stewardship, just as discipleship is the only kind of Christianity (Luke 9:23-24). Nothing short of total surrender meets the biblical requirement. "No man can face earnestly the challenge of Jesus of Nazareth without discovering that all of life—all that a man is and has—is a gift of God" (Thomas, 1946, p. 9).

Having established the all-encompassing nature of stewardship, this article will now narrow its focus to parenting (Ephesians 6:4). It will establish that parents are stewards of their children. God is the giver of life and the owner of all living creatures. Children are not given to parents as possessions; they are entrusted to parents for safe-keeping and godly training (Deuteronomy 6:7-9, Proverbs 22:6).

Parenting Is Stewardship

Parenting is like planting trees. Bible teacher John MacArthur (2000) asserts that Christian parents are called to plant trees that will provide shade to future generations; "shade that will protect others from the blistering heat of an anti-Christian society" (p. 3). Parenting is a precious trust. "Only a little child, you say. Yet within that little mind and body there is the possibility of influence upon the entire world. Children are a mighty stewardship for parents who have once known the call of God in Christ" (Thomas, 1946, p. 52). Thomas (1946) powerfully illustrates parenting as stewardship through the story of a widow in India who once wrote on a pledge card: "I will give to Christ six *annas* and my baby boy." Years later after richly investing in her sons life, he graduated from college and theological school and became one of the great preachers in the church in India (p. 52).

Parents who see themselves as stewards consider parental influence part of stewardship. "Every human being is responsible both to God and to his fellowman. Just as every tree casts its shadow, so every man has influence. Good or bad, our deeds follow us" (McKay, 1974, p. 73). Whatever platform of influence Christians have is a gift from God, consequently children are the first recipients of their Christian parents' influence. Whether that influence is godly or worldly, children observe, absorb, and imitate the choices of their parents. "A man may die, but his influence lives on" (McKay, 1974, p. 78).

The Stewardship of the Gospel

Christian parents are recipients of the gift of eternal life. Their knowledge and experience of Christ as Savior is an aspect of Christian stewardship. God expects Christian parents to share their understanding of and belief in the gospel with their children. The mission of presenting the gospel to children begins with an understanding that regeneration is the child's greatest need and that fulfilling the great commission begins at home (Matthew 28:19-20) (MacArthur, 2000). While it is a sign of good parenting to meet the physical and educational needs of children, the need for salvation must be every Christian parent's priority. Children must be taught important doctrinal truths, such as the holiness of God (Leviticus 11:44-45), the sinfulness of man (Romans 7:13), the sacrifice of Christ on the cross (Ephesians 1:7), the cost of discipleship (Mark10:21) and the need to accept the gift of eternal life that God offers through His Son (2 Corinthians 5:11) (MacArthur, 2000).

One common mistake that well-meaning Christian parents make is assuming that their children are born again. A well-behaved, compliant child might be mistaken for a genuine believer. However, Farley (2009) emphasizes that the new birth does not equal to church attendance or youth group involvement. New birth is the result of a supernatural act of God. "It is radical, revolutionary and lasting" (Farley, 2009, p. 29). God-centered parents do not parent for this life; instead they "labor to prepare each child for the Day of Judgment. The stakes are inexpressibly high" (Farley, 2009, p. 41).

The Stewardship of Biblical Authority

Jesus' life on earth was characterized by obedience to the Father. In John 5:30, Jesus declares: "I can do nothing on my own authority." Bible teacher Charles Kraft (1997) declares, "Jesus' intimacy with the Father enabled him to maintain his authority and to get God's instructions concerning what the Father wanted Him to do each day" (p. 36.) As one under authority, Jesus passed on His authority to His followers. This powerful gift demands responsible stewardship. Believers do not own God-given authority, but they can use it rightly and without presumption (Kraft, 1997). The use of this powerful weapon calls for an utter dependence on the Holy Spirit, a life totally surrendered to the authority of the Lord Jesus Christ and an attitude of service, humility, and love (Kraft, 1997). According to Kraft (1997), ignoring the balance between believers' allegiance to Christ, love for His truth, and powerful use of His authority is the reason why so many Christians live in defeat. Parents have the authority to bless and discipline their children.

The authority to bless children. Children yearn for approval. The unconditional love and approval of their parents is a prized possession. Many adults who grew up in homes where words of love, affirmation, and blessing were never spoken carry with them lasting wounds (Smalley, 1993). The power of blessings is repeatedly illustrated in the Old Testament. Dramatic family stories where a father's blessing on his children determined the child's destiny cannot be underestimated (Genesis 27, 48). Kraft (1997) declares, "Invoking God's blessing on those you favor was, for the Jews, almost as natural as breathing" (p. 225). God's emphasis on words of blessing is included in the Scripture for a reason. The authority to bless is a precious gift because "genuine spiritual transactions take place when we speak blessings in Jesus' name" (Kraft, 1997, p. 225). Blessing children involves meaningful touch such as hugs and kisses and a spoken message of blessing, affirmation, and high value (Smalley, 1993). Blessing also includes picturing a bright future for the child and a commitment on the part of parents to make that bright future a reality (Smalley, 1993). Smalley (1993) concludes that a blessing is always intentional; "a blessing becomes so only when it is spoken" (p. 19). Blessings taken out of Scripture (1 Chronicles 4:10, Numbers 6:24-26, Psalms 1, 23, 91, 112, 139, Philippians 1) and pronounced on children reap incalculable fruit in the life of the child and the Kingdom of God.

The authority to discipline children. Children are commanded to obey their parents (Exodus 20:12) and parents are commanded to discipline their children (Prov. 19:18). Parental authority demands responsible stewardship and obedience to God on the part of parents. Children begin life as enemies of God (Younts, 2004). They must contend externally with a world pressuring them to conform to ungodliness and internally with the curse of sin (MacArthur, 2000). Psalm 51:5 declares: "Surely I was sinful at birth, sinful from the time my mother conceived me" (New International Version, NIV). Understanding children's bent toward sin, which clearly points to their need for the gospel, is fundamental for parents. The gospel and discipline are therefore, inseparable. The relevance of the gospel convinces parents that sin is the problem and that parental authority is crucial. Godly discipline presents an opportunity to explain the gospel to children by pursuing their hearts and not just their behavior (Jeremiah 17:9) (Farley, 2009). MacArthur (2000) states that learning obedience to parents early in life sets the stage for obedience to God throughout life. MacArthur (2000) emphasizes that if parents fail to discipline their children, God will.

If discipline is seen as an opportunity to teach children the truth of the gospel, then the message is not complete without an understanding of grace. Biblical discipline is always administered in the context of love, not anger. The lavished affection of parents and their unconditional love for children is the surest way to show them the love of God. When parents make their own feelings of disappointment, hurt, or anger the central focus of discipline, the opportunity of teaching children the saving power of the gospel is compromised (Younts, 2004). Discipline and an attitude of grace must be inseparable. Children need constant reminders of the grace and love of God because they fail often, just like their parents. Children can be taught the importance of honoring God's authority and trusting God's loving and merciful nature.

Teaching Children the Stewardship of Time

The focus of this article now turns to aspects of stewardship children must learn from their parents. The first aspect that will be explored is the stewardship of time. Time is a resource. "It cannot be accumulated like money or stockpiled like raw materials. We are forced to spend it whether we choose it or not, at a fixed rate of 60 seconds every minute. It cannot be turned on and off like a machine. It is irretrievable" (Keathley, 2010, p.). Time is a precious gift that demands responsible stewardship. In an age when there are so many distractions competing for the attention of children, it is crucial for parents to teach and model a God-honoring use of time.

The Value of Work

One way to appreciate the value of time is to teach children to appreciate diligence and hard work. In *20 Rules and Tools for a Great Family,* Steven Stephens (2006) asserts that children benefit greatly when their parents teach them the importance of work. Among other benefits, hard work "builds a can-do attitude, teaches responsibility, develops skills, overcomes laziness, enriches character, strengthens self-esteem and keeps children out of trouble" (Stephens, 2006, p. 62). Work is an effective way for young people to learn self-discipline. Work helps them to develop priorities. It encourages them to eliminate excuses and to focus on reaping rewards once the job is complete (Maxwell, 1999).

One way to instill a strong work ethic in children is to teach them what the Bible says about diligence (Proverbs 13:4). "Lazy hands make a man poor, but diligent hands bring wealth" (Proverbs 12:24, NIV). Diligence brings forth reward. "The plans of the diligent lead to profit as surely as haste leads to poverty" (Proverbs 21:5, NIV). Diligence conjures up the image of going "after something with determination, passion and skill with a final goal in mind. Diligence is such an important virtue that the person who develops it can stand before kings (Prov. 22:29)" (Stone, 2009, p. 174). Teaching young people what the Bible says about hard work is not enough; diligence must be modeled by parents. Working with a cheerful spirit and without complaining should be the hallmark of all the members of the family (Philippians 2:14-15).

Through everyday chores children can learn the benefits of work. Parents must teach them early on in life how they can contribute to the well-being of the entire family. It is also necessary to teach children how to do certain chores. Jobs must be age appropriate and done routinely. Work can be a joyful experience when children are taught with a positive attitude, when teamwork is encouraged, and when perfection is not expected (Stephens, 2006). Maxwell (1999) declares, "I have yet to find the man, however exalted his station, who did not do better work and put forth a greater effort under a spirit of approval than under a spirit of criticism" (p. 8).

The Value of Reading

One way to instill the value of time early in life is to introduce children to the pleasure and delight of reading. Children are always learning and being influenced. That influence is either good or bad. Influence is never neutral (Younts, 2004). As stewards, parents are the gatekeepers of the influence their children receive through television, videos, movies, computer games, the Internet, friends, music, and books. Instead of focusing on the negative effects of media, this article will focus on the benefits of reading. How can parents instill a love for learning and reading in their children? Reading benefits children enormously. According to Stephens (2006) reading widens their horizons, it stimulates their imagination, it counters the influence of television, it encourages the discovery of new interests, it enhances academic achievement, it strengthens family togetherness, and it provides fond memories.

Having considered these benefits, parents can do a lot to encourage reading at home. Stephens (2006) believes that the first step is to turn off the TV, which "increases passivity, obesity, anxiety and aggressiveness; it also decreases creativity and social interaction" (p. 124). The second step is to foster a love for reading. Parents can do that by reading themselves, reading to children (beginning at birth), choosing reading material carefully, making books accessible to children of all ages (starting a library), listening to audio books, taking children to the library and bookstores, expressing excitement about reading, and getting children books for birthdays and Christmas as special gifts (Stephens, 2006). Good books must be well-written and their literary style should appeal to readers and hold their attention. Good books must be enjoyed. They must not be too easy or too hard to read. Good books can be narrated (Cooper, 2004).

Reading aloud to children is a great gift. Parents can create these special moments with their children by setting up a time and place and by carefully choosing good books. Reading aloud will not only benefit language acquisition and reading ability, but it can also be a valuable opportunity to teach Bible stories, theological concepts in simple terms, and values that build character.

Teaching Children the Stewardship of Talent

Children are talented, skilled, and gifted. One of the greatest joys that parenting offers is the opportunity to help children discover their strengths, talents, and spiritual gifts. No matter how young children are, they can be taught "when the commonplace is accepted as a stewardship, even the most meager talents contribute a mighty influence upon the world" (Thomas, 1946, p. 47). Once those talents are identified, parents must teach children how to be wise stewards of those talents and encourage them to use their strengths and gifts for the glory of God.

Parents can remind their children that even small talents are significant. When gifts are used, God multiplies them and strengthens them (McKay, 1974). Parents must also remind children that big talents are to be used for God glory and not one's vanity. Talents belong to God. He owns them (McKay, 1974). Wise stewards recognize that God deserves all the credit. A day of reckoning is coming when all will give an account to the Owner and Giver of all talents (McKay, 1974). "Miracles occur every day. One can occur in the life of any person [child] whose talents are held as a sacred stewardship, to be used wisely for God's work in the world" (Thomas, 1946, p. 52).

Throughout this article the importance of setting an example for children has been emphasized. In the area of talents and service, this principle is also true. Children will develop a desire to minister to others from parents who model empathy and compassion for others. Because children tend to be self-centered and self-absorbed, it is up to parents to alert them of the needs of others and encourage them to serve. Children who are loved and cared for learn to love and care for others. Fuller (2001) asserts that when children's "emotional cups are full of love from parents and others around them, the more they are able to love others" (p. 174).

Children and Spiritual Gifts

Parents and teachers spend a lot of time telling children to sit still and be quiet. However it is important to teach them how to be active as well. To engage children in ministry is vital to their spiritual formation (Carr, 2008). The Bible declares that God's children are created for good works (Ephesians 2:10) and that spiritual gifts have been bestowed to every believer (Romans 12:3-8). Service opportunities during childhood teach the importance of volunteerism and the rewards of ministry. The joys of service can and must be learned early in life (Carr, 2008).

Parents can help their children identify their spiritual gifts by observing the activities children like the most. For example, parents might observe a child's desire to study the Bible, or his or her leadership ability, or a tendency to feel the pain of others, or an inclination toward service. By helping children to recognize their spiritual gifts, parents can provide them with a healthy sense of worth and a great source of joy. Even one talent used for God's glory can yield significant fruit for the Kingdom of God.

Teaching Children the Stewardship of Treasure

The strong influence toward materialism and individualism characteristic of this era presents a seemingly insurmountable challenge for Christian parents who want to teach their children the biblical stewardship of treasure. However difficult it will be, parents will be called upon to take a counter-cultural stance in order to succeed as godly parents. Parenting educator Jim Fay (2010) has authored a book called *From Innocence to Entitlement*. During a presentation to parents, he shared the event that inspired him to write such a book. A teenager came to his counseling practice. She was convinced that all her misery was her parents' fault whose "grave" mistake was to decide they would not buy her a two-door convertible. It was impossible for her to fathom that her parents did not understand she was entitled to such a privilege (Fay, 2010).

Thomas (1946) asserts, "A large portion of the progress of individuals and society can be traced to the inspiration of hardship" (p. 32). Adversity, financial limitations, and defeat often bring out the best in individuals and nations (Thomas, 1946). The opposite can also be true. While previous generations took great pleasure in simple blessings and worked hard to achieve their goals, younger generations born to luxury tend to take affluence, opportunity, and success for granted (Thomas, 1946). Having received every privilege and material possession without effort on their part, they have become ungrateful and spoiled.

Young people under the age of thirty are considered the "Me Generation" or "GenMe" by researcher Jean Twenge (2006). Characteristic of this generation is an emphasis on materialism and a tendency to measure success in terms of having a lot of money (Twenge, 2006). The fact that, like never before, young people are targeted by aggressive marketing and advertisement campaigns makes them vulnerable to an unbiblical view of financial stewardship. Today's culture teaches children that they are entitled to an abundance of expensive toys just because they are special (Twenge, 2006). According to Twenge (2006) the high expectations children have concerning possessions and status make this generation of young people the most susceptible to anxiety, depression, and loneliness. This proves that materialism does not satisfy (Mark 8:36).

The essential ingredient to developing "fruitful lives and sterling character" is biblical stewardship (Thomas, 1946, p. 37). Children who suffer hardship are often grateful for small blessings and are conscious of others who are less fortunate. Therefore, children who are born privileged must be intentionally taught these virtues. "Only a consecrated spirit of stewardship" can produce them (Thomas, 1946, p. 37). Opportunity and affluence are a trust. Children must learn at a young age that an abundance of blessings equals abundant responsibility (Luke 12:48).

Financial Principles Children Can Learn

The best way for parents to teach their children biblical financial principles is to model them. Children take note when parents practice self-control, write a tithe check, and give generously to missions and the needy. Parents who believe that God is the owner of everything live accordingly and teach their children the following principles.

Parents can teach their children to associate money with labor. They should help their children to understand that financial profit results from hard work (Alcorn, 1989). According to Randy Alcorn (1989), handing money to children teaches them that money has no cost. Parents can be the teachers of a strong work ethic and diligence by teaching their children that unwise financial decisions have consequences (Burkett & Osborn, 1996). When children make a foolish purchase that later prevents them from buying what they really want, parents should allow those consequences to run their course (Galatians 6:8) (Alcorn, 1989).

Teaching children the importance of saving money provides a major lesson on self-control and discipline (Proverbs 21:5) (Alcorn, 1989). Children also learn wisdom and responsibility when they are asked to save enough money to make a big purchase instead of getting it on credit (Burkett & Osborn, 1996). Buying immediately as the desire arises is often based on feelings of impulsivity. When children walk away from an item and instead make a savings plan to acquire it, they learn the value of money (Burkett & Osborn, 1996). When the item is finally purchased, the value of each dollar is truly understood and the item is appreciated more fully.

Teaching children budgeting skills is essential to learning other important skills such as time management and life management (Burkett & Osborn, 1996). It allows children to appreciate the concept of time and finances. Dividing money into categories helps them to learn the importance of planning and prioritizing (Burkett & Osborn, 1996). Having a budget also shows them the freedom that results from allotting certain amounts of money to specific expenses. Budgeting fosters self-control and discipline (Matthew 6:19-21, 33).

Teaching children the priority of tithing emphasizes that giving is a habit and like all good habits it must be cultivated (Alcorn, 1989). Alcorn (1989) believes that tithing is a holy habit just like Bible study, prayer, witnessing, and hospitality. One way to foster this holy habit is to give children three jars with the following designations: giving, savings, and spending. Whenever they get paid they are instructed to deposit at least 10% of their earnings in the giving jar (Malachi 3:10). Once an amount has been deposited in the giving jar, it cannot be taken out; that money becomes sacred and it belongs to the Lord (Alcorn, 1989).

Lastly, parents can teach their children the joy of giving by encouraging them to give to missions and the needy (Proverbs 28:27). Generous parents beget generous children. Few blessings compare to the joy of giving so others will hear the gospel, so a poor child in a foreign land can get a warm meal a day, or so a loved one will be encouraged and ministered to by a timely gift. Families who practice generosity will agree with missionary Hudson Taylor when he said: "The less I spent on myself and the more I gave to others, the fuller of happiness and blessing did my soul become (Alcorn, 1989, p. 393).

Implications for Children's Ministry

Why is teaching parents these important truths about parenting and stewardship so important? Ham & Beemer (2009) report, "61% of today's young adults who were regular church attendees are now 'spiritually disengaged.' They are not attending church, praying, or reading their Bibles" (p. 24). This staggering statistic shows that taking children to church on Sunday morning is not enough for them to have real faith in Christ. In order for children's ministry to be effective and biblical, it must reach out to parents by reminding them of and equipping them to fulfill their role as priests in their home (Deuteronomy 6:4-9). An analogy can be drawn from the cast of a movie where parents are the main characters in children's spiritual lives while children's ministers and volunteers are supporting actors.

George Barna (2007) in his book, *Revolutionary Parenting: What the Research Shows Really Works*, declares, "if my children are going to grow spiritually, most of that growth will come from what takes place inside the house" (p. 152). He goes on to say that this kind of parenting does not come naturally, but must be intentional. In the same way, reaching out to parents and teaching them biblical principles of parenting is of paramount importance and needs to be intentional as well.

Some suggestions include teaching parents the all-encompassing nature of stewardship and its relationship to Christian parenting through parenting conferences or seminars. The importance of blessing children could be taught as such seminars. *A Father's Guide to Blessing His Children* by

Children Desiring God Ministries is an excellent resource for parents. It includes the biblical basis for blessing children and provides examples of blessing prayers. The subject of discipline is popular among parents, and seminars on discipline are usually well-attended. During these seminars a brief introduction to the subject of discipline as it relates to stewardship and authority would provide a biblical context for the importance of godly discipline in the home.

The stewardship of time, talent, and treasure could be taught to parents and their children together. Practical ideas for fostering the stewardship of time would be to encourage family book clubs. *The Chronicles of Narnia* and missionary biographies would be excellent selections. The stewardship of talent can be introduced by offering workshops where parents and their children (both) identify their spiritual gifts. Additionally, parents and their children could learn about serving opportunities for the entire family. Ministry Tools Resource Center provides helpful ways of encouraging children to discover their spiritual gifts. Lastly, the stewardship of treasure can be instilled by introducing parents and their children to the jar system previously mentioned. Crown Financial Ministries offer excellent resources for parents to teach their children.

Conclusion

Thomas (1946) reflects, "Jesus came teaching stewardship. He used the words 'steward' and 'stewardship' to enable his followers to get a clear picture of their privilege and responsibility as recipients of the gifts of God" (p. 14). Among life's most precious God-given gifts are the children entrusted to parents. Steward-parents invest their lives for the well-being of their children. They see their offspring as a valuable trust and family life as a "crucible for holiness" (Mohler, 2010).

References

Alcorn, R. (1989). *Money, possessions, and eternity.* Wheaton, IL: Tyndale House.

Barna, G. (2007). *Revolutionary parenting: What the research shows really works.* Carol Stream, IL: Tyndale House.

Burkett, L., & Risk, O. (1996). *Financial parenting.* Colorado Springs, CO: Chariot Victor.

Burney, L. (2004). *Super foods for healthy kids.* New York, NY: Sterling.

Carr, J. (2008) *Nurturing children's spirituality.* Edited by Holly Allen. Eugene, OR: Cascade Books.

Cooper, E. (2004). *When children love to learn.* Wheaton, IL: Crossway Books.

Farley, W. (2009). *Gospel-powered parenting.* Phillipsburg, NJ: P&R.

Fay, J. "From innocence to entitlement." Retrieved from http://www.youtube.com/watch?v=tZ7e3fhYI_w.

Fuller, C. (2001). *Opening your child's spiritual windows.* Grand Rapids, MI: Zondervan.

Ham, K., & Britt, B. (2009). *Already gone: Why your kids will quit church and what you can do to stop it.* Green Forest, AR: New Leaf.

Jeremiah, D. *Stewardship is lordship* [CD]. San Diego, CA: Turning Point.

Keathley, H. "The stewardship of time." Retrieved from http://bible.org/seriespage/stewardship-time.

Kraft, C. (1997). *I give you authority.* Grand Rapids, MI: Baker.

MacArthur, J. (2000). *What the Bible says about parenting: God's plan for rearing your child.* Nashville, TN: Word.

Maxwell, J. (1999). *The 21 indispensable qualities of a leader.* Nashville, TN: Thomas Nelson.

McKay, C. (1974). *The spirit-filled steward.* Nashville, TN: Convention Press.

McMahon, M. "Christian stewardship." Retrieved from http://www.apuritansmind.com/Stewardship/StewardMainPage.htm; Internet.

Mohler, A. "Why are parents so unhappy?" Retrieved from http://www.albertmohler.com/2010/07/08/why-are-parents-so-unhappy-and-who-would-settle-for-happiness-anyway.

Smalley, G., & Trent, J. (1993). *The gift of the blessing*. Nashville, TN: Thomas Nelson.

Stephens, S. (2006). *20 rules and tools for a great family*. Carol Stream, IL: Tyndale House.

Stone, P. (2009) *Breaking the Jewish code: 12 secrets that will transform your life, family, health, and finances*. Lake Mary, FL: Charisma House.

Thomas, E. (1946). *To whom much is given*. New York, NY: Abingdon-Cokesbury Press.

Twenge, J. (2006). *Generation me: Why today's young Americans are more confident, assertive, entitled, and more miserable than ever before*. New York, NY: Free Press.

Younts, J. (2004) *Everyday talk*. Wapwallopen, PA: Shepherd Press.

Author Biography

Dr. Sudi Gliebe is a Professor of Family Ministry at B. H. Carroll Institute in Arlington, Texas.

A Biblical Theology for the 4/14 Window Based Upon Deuteronomy 6

Steven R. Entsminger

Abstract: This paper examines the demographic concept of the 4/14 Window, children between the ages of four and fourteen, and the instructions given by Moses to the Israelites in Deuteronomy 6. This text contains the *Shema*, which specifically charges the Israelite parents and instructs them how to teach the commandments of God to their children. God's plan, as seen throughout the Scriptures, has been for parents to instruct their children in the commands of God. God promised His blessings as generation to generation loved and obeyed Him. But neglect and disobedience brought disaster upon Israel. Today, God's people need to heed the instruction of Deuteronomy 6, taking special care to train the children, to avoid similar disaster.

Children have a prominent role throughout Scripture. Studies show that children are open and responsive to the Gospel. Due to their number and susceptibility to suffering, they represent the most needy of the Gospel. They also present the greatest opportunity for life transformation not only in themselves, but also in the world. The largest harvest field in the world consists of the children between the ages of four and fourteen, a golden window of opportunity, thus the missiological term "the 4/14 Window."

This paper will examine the 4/14 Window as a biblical theology in light of Deuteronomy 6. It will give a brief history and overview of the 4/14 Window movement, view the *Shema* section of Deuteronomy 6 for biblical insights, observe the intention of the Lord, review further instructions found in Deuteronomy, and Israel's failure with their children.

Explanation of the 4/14 Window

In 1994, Dan Brewster coined the demographic concept of the 4/14 Window in his published article, "The 4/14 Window: Child Ministries and Mission Strategy." This built upon the geographical concept of Luis Bush's 10/40 Window (Gonzales, 2012). Both Brewster and Bush continued to write and promote the 4/14 Window strategy throughout the world to the point that this strategy exists as the 4/14 Movement where leaders and practitioners in many countries form a fraternity of proponents for children and their place in the kingdom of God.

Studies show that children before the age of fifteen are the most open group of people to the Gospel. George Barna (2003) discovered that "the probability of someone embracing Jesus as his or her Savior was 32 percent for those between the ages of 5 and 12; 4 percent for those in the 13-to-18-age range; and 6 percent for people 19 or older" (p. 34). He concluded that if one does not hear and choose to follow Christ as Savior before their mid-teen years, they most likely never will.

The 4/14 Movement pursues a four-fold focus: 1) reach into the world to serve and love this generation; 2) rescue children from oppression, deception, depression, and destruction; 3) root children in Christ the sustainer of all things, the nurturer of their souls; and 4) release them into the fields to reap the greatest harvest in history (What Is the 4/14 Window? 2013). These foci represent a holistic approach to minister to those of the 4/14 Window.

The *Shema* in Deuteronomy 6

Deuteronomy records the final days of Moses as the leader of the people of Israel. He obeyed God as Israel's deliverer from slavery in Egypt to take them to the Promised Land in fulfillment to the promise made to Abraham, Isaac, and Jacob. Israel refused to trust God and enter the land for which they suffered forty years of punishment wandering in the desert. At the presentation of Deuteronomy, Israel was soon to enter the Promised Land. The unfaithful generation died off, the new generation prepared to cross the Jordan River.

Moses spoke to this new generation and recapitulated the commandments and decrees given by the Lord previously. He made "a call for total
devotion to Yahweh" and to make sound spiritual choices as did Abraham
before them (McIntosh & Anders, 2002, p. 4). Moses gave the new generation about to enter the land one final review of the commands, statutes,
and rules for them to succeed as the called people of God. "It is to be a
deep, moving, all-consuming, whole-souled love for God that prompts Israel to keep his commandments and communicate them to their children"
(Oberst, 1968, p. 108).

Deuteronomy 6 provided the basic principles for the Jewish people.
The entire book pivots on this chapter and includes the *Shema* that consists in the Great Commandment, which declares the Lord as one (Miller,
1990). Jews recite it to affirm their faith and make confession to the Lord.
Jewish children learn the *Shema* as a primary passage of Scripture and recite it every morning and evening (Oberst, 1968). Jesus declared it as the
greatest commandment when questioned by one of the teachers of the law
(Mark 12:28-31).

Deuteronomy 6:1-9 reads:

> Now this is the commandment—the statutes and the rules—that
> the LORD your God commanded me to teach you, that you may
> do them in the land to which you are going over, to possess it, that
> you may fear the LORD your God, you and your son and your son's
> son, by keeping all his statutes and his commandments, which I
> command you, all the days of your life, and that your days may
> be long. Hear therefore, O Israel, and be careful to do them, that
> it may go well with you, and that you may multiply greatly, as
> the LORD, the God of your fathers, has promised you, in a land
> flowing with milk and honey. "Hear, O Israel: The LORD our God,
> the LORD is one You shall love the LORD your God with all your
> heart and with all your soul and with all your might. And these
> words that I command you today shall be on your heart. [7] You
> shall teach them diligently to your children, and shall talk of them
> when you sit in your house, and when you walk by the way, and
> when you lie down, and when you rise. You shall bind them as
> a sign on your hand, and they shall be as frontlets between your

eyes. You shall write them on the doorposts of your house and on your gates (English Standard Version, ESV).

Moses exhorted the new generation entering the Promised Land to whole-heartily love and obey God. He challenged them to embrace the covenant agreement made forty years earlier, which their parents refused to do, suffered greatly for their disobedience, and died outside the Promised Land.

The text makes a generational emphasis on two different occasions in stating "you [fathers], your son and your son's son" (vs. 2) and "your children" (vs. 7). The current fathers received instruction from their fathers, and some, those who were less than twenty years of age, actually received those instructions directly from the Lord. The new generation carried the responsibility to teach love for God and obedience of His commands to their children, who would replicate the teaching to their children in order to propagate the missional purposes of Israel as the chosen nation of God. "The future of Israel depends on the transmission of the experience of God's mighty act in history and His demands to each successive generation" (Christensen, 2001, p. 81).

These verses focus on the children, who represented the next generations. "The effective passing on of the central components of the covenant was crucial to the continuance and health of the covenant community in its relationship with God" (Hall, 2000, p. 134). The Lord's intention throughout the Scripture required parents to instruct their children who in turn instruct their children so they might obey the Lord and so it would go well with them.

Intention of God

The plan of God has continually been for fathers to teach by word and example to their children a love for and obedience to God. God's blessing and command in Genesis 1:28, "be fruitful and multiply" to Adam and Eve infers the reproduction of human beings providing the effective means to "fill" the earth (Castleberry, 2009, p. 11). Thus parenthood provided the need to instruct the children about the commandments of the Lord and to tell of their history with Him.

Genesis 6:1 recorded that "man began to multiply on the face of the land" but "the Lord saw that the wickedness of man was great in the earth" (vs. 5, ESV). The proper instruction of offspring from the time of Adam and Eve proved insufficient and lacking to the point that the Lord decided to "blot out man" (vs. 7) except for one man. Noah knew the Lord, walked with Him, and was considered a righteous man, blameless in his generation. God saved Noah and his immediate family through the building of the ark. Upon leaving the ark, Noah built the first altar and offered a burnt sacrifice that pleased the Lord. Thus the Lord renewed the blessing and command of Genesis 1:28. The Lord commanded Noah and his sons to be fruitful, to multiply and to fill the earth (9:1). This once again inferred reproduction, which required proper instruction in the story and relationship with the Lord to the offspring (Keil and Delitzsch, E-sword HD Electronic Bible). Noah and his sons demonstrated obedience to the reproduction command and Genesis 11 and 12 recount the nations that resulted from their efforts.

The next major shift in the intention of God is seen in the life of Abram as the narrative moves from the Lord dealing with all nations to "the patriarchal narrative" (Wright, 2006, p. 194). Israel emerged as a nation or a people with whom the Lord sought to fulfill His desire to bless all nations. The Lord instructed Abram to leave his country, people, and family and to go to a new land. The command came with a promise (Genesis 12:2), "and I will make of you a great nation." The Lord reinforced the promise by stating, "To your offspring I will give this land" (vs. 7) thus implying reproduction, which would again require instruction and history in the relationship with the Lord.

The narrative continued through the life of Abraham to Isaac where the Lord appeared to Isaac with the promise of His presence, blessing, and increase of children (Genesis 26:24). Isaac's son Jacob received a similar appearance and promise from the Lord (Genesis 28:13-15). Jacob's twelve sons resulted in the twelve tribes of Israel redeemed from Egypt under the leadership of Moses in the book of Exodus. Upon arrival to Mount Sinai, the Lord spoke to Moses expressing His promise and desire for Israel, found in Exodus 19:5-6, "Now therefore, if you will indeed obey my voice and keep my covenant, you shall be my treasured possession among all peoples, for all the earth is mine; and you shall be to me a kingdom of priests and a holy nation. These are the words that you shall speak to the people of Israel" (ESV). In order for Israel to fulfill the promise and desire of God as priests and nation, the sacredness and calling demanded an instruction of the next generations.

Within the narrative of the people of Israel, Aaron, his sons, and "his offspring after him" (Exodus 28:43) received anointing, ordination, and consecration to serve the Lord as priests. Specific clothing, responsibilities, and actions were explicitly given to the priests as servants before the Lord. Each generation of priests taught the next generation as part of their responsibilities. Their anointing admitted them to a perpetual priesthood throughout their generations (Exodus 40:15). The promise included the offspring of Aaron but required faithful, diligent, effective instruction of the next generation.

Joseph Castleberry (2009) writes from a perspective of migration but also includes reproduction in his paper which states that standard biblical theologies of missions not only lack discussion of Genesis 1:28, but also omit "any discussion whatsoever of either reproduction or migration—the two main vehicles by which the Gospel has been spread throughout the history of Israel and the Church" (p. 4).

A brief review of the references from Genesis to Deuteronomy clearly shows that God's intention in relationship to humankind flows from generation to generation. Parents participate through telling of the story of the Lord's instruction and intervention. Deuteronomy continues with the need and responsibility of parents to teach their children in the ways of the Lord.

Instructions in Deuteronomy

In Deuteronomy 4, Moses cried out to the nation of Israel to listen and obey the statutes and rules God gave them. If they listened and obeyed they would live, go in, and take possession of the Promised Land (vs. 1). Moses repeatedly pleaded with them to keep the statutes and rules of the Lord in order for them to live and for it to go well with them. He cautioned them to take care, to remember the things that they had seen with their eyes, and not to let them depart from their heart (vs. 9). They were "to make them known to their children and their children's children" (vs. 9, ESV). They were to teach them, diligently (Deuteronomy 6:7, 11:19). "[T]heir obligation [was] to imbue the minds of the young and rising generation with similar sentiments of reverence and respect for it [the law]" (Jamieson, Fausset, and Brown, E-sword HD Electronic Bible).

The Israelite adults of the new generation first needed a place for the commands of God in their own heart and then to transmit them to their children (Deuteronomy 6:6). The Lord gave the commands directly to the adults with the expectation that they would first keep, guard, and practice them. Through their obedience and faithfulness the generations (their children and their children's children) would see and seek to follow in their ways of obedience to the Lord.

The Law told Fathers to teach the commands of the Lord diligently to their children as the priests and the nation of God, who would soon instill them to their children. Orberst (1968) translated this phrase, "You shall whet *and* sharpen them, so as to make them penetrate, *and* teach *and* impress them diligently upon the minds (and hearts) of your children" (p. 108). The *Torah* demanded that the statutes and rules of the Lord be impressed upon their minds and hearts. "It is expressive of diligence and industry in teaching, by frequent repetition of things, by inculcating them continually into their minds, endeavouring to imprint them there, that they may be sharp, ready, and expert in them" (Gill, E-sword HD Electronic Bible). The Lord asked for His people to take seriously and accomplish with great diligence the instruction of His ways to the next generation.

The Lord wanted parents to simply talk about Him to their children each day as opportunity presented itself. "Moses thought his law so very plain and easy that every father might be able to instruct his sons in it and every mother her daughters. Thus that good thing which is committed to us we must carefully transmit to those that come after us, that it may be perpetuated" (Henry, E-sword HD Electronic Bible). Moses encouraged them to talk about the Lord while sitting at home, while walking along the road, when lying down in the evening, or getting up in the morning (Deuteronomy 6:7b, 11:19). In the day-to-day tasks and activities of life,

Deuteronomy instructed parents to teach their children about the Lord's statutes, rules, and history.

Parents needed not only to talk to their children, but also to employ physical objects as well. "You shall bind them as a sign on your hand, and they shall be as frontlets between your eyes. You shall write them on the doorposts of your house and on your gates" (Deuteronomy 6:8-9, ESV). Jewish families literally obeyed this command with the use of *phylacteries* and *mezuzahs*. Priests wrote Deuteronomy 6:4-9 and 11:13-20 on small parchments and placed them in leather pouches (*phylacteries*) and tied them to a person's hand, arm, or between his or her eyes. They also placed the parchments in small boxes called *mezuzahs* and hung them on the doorway of the home. As fathers entered and left the home they would touch the box, kiss their finger, and speak a benediction. This as well as prayers of the family, weekly Sabbath attendance, and participation in festive seasons impressed themselves upon the mind of the child (Edersheim, E-sword HD Electronic Bible).

The regular activities and conversations in the family would provoke the inquisitive minds of their children to question their parents. "When your son asks you in time to come, 'What is the meaning of the testimonies and the statutes and the rules that the LORD our God has commanded you?' then you shall say to your son, 'We were Pharaoh›s slaves in Egypt. And the LORD brought us out of Egypt with a mighty hand'" (Deuteronomy 6:20-21, ESV). As the children observed the diligence of their parents in keeping the commandments of the Lord, as they lived well in the land, the children would question, "Why?" This would provide an opportunity once again to tell the story of the Lord's great deliverance and promise. The Lord used this practice regularly with the Israelites.

God commanded the Passover rite, as instituted in Exodus 12, as a statute that would last forever. When the Israelites celebrated the rite each year in the Promised Land, it allowed for the children in the following generations to question the purpose of the celebration. "What do you mean by this service" (Exodus 12:26). This provided opportunity for their fathers to describe the events of the Lord's deliverance from slavery in Egypt and their place in the mission of God.

Joshua reproduced this upon crossing the Jordan River in Joshua 4. As the Israelites crossed the Jordan River on dry ground, Joshua instructed that each tribe provide a man to remove a stone from the riverbed where the priests' stood. They laid the twelve stones together as a monument for the next generations. When the children saw the stones and asked, "What do these stones mean to you?" (Joshua 4:6), the story of the Lord going before the Israelites as they took possession of the Promised Land would be told by their parents, once again affirming their role as the people of God.

God's intention clearly demonstrates His desire that fathers, with the community in general as well, give instruction and formation to the children given to him by God. Today, the local church plays a dynamic role in this process as well. Brewster (2011) quotes Douglas McConnell in *Understanding God's Heart for Children*:

> Children are essential to the life and ministry of the church, bringing spiritual gifts and abilities and fulfilling definite roles. The church needs to be a place where children may dynamically connect with God and engage in meaningful participation; discipled, equipped, and empowered for life and ministry. As members of the family of God, children are to be cared for as sons and daughters and are part of the admonition to love and serve one another. God intends for churches to provide children with opportunities to know Him and fulfill their calling in the body of Christ (p. 108).

Once again Deuteronomy 6 shows that God's interest lies particularly in a love for Him with all the heart, soul, and might in order to fulfill the destiny and mission of God in the lives of every person beginning in their childhood. Children have a purpose to fulfill in the kingdom of God and play a principal role in the narrative of the mission of God. Children require instruction, training, and formation in their impressionable years, to fulfill that mission God ordained them to accomplish.

Failure

The Lord promised the land, His presence, and blessing to the second generation of Israelites freed from Egyptian slavery. The Lord simply wanted them to live in the land, obey Him, and teach the same to their offspring. This assured a good, long life and a witness to the nations. Israel failed in their commitment to the Lord. The book of Judges recounted the back and forth relationship of Israel with the Lord. Joshua and his generation, those "who had seen all the great work that the LORD had done for Israel" (Judges 2:7, ESV) died. A whole other generation arose who did not know the Lord nor the many things He had done for Israel (Judges 2:10). They suffered greatly because the parents did not properly instruct them about the Lord, His commands, nor what He had done in the past for them.

Throughout the history of Israel in the Old Testament the failure of parents in teaching their children the ways of the Lord proved disastrous. Kings, priests, and false prophets arose that led the Israelites in idolatry. The depravity of some parents allowed them to sacrifice their children to false gods (Jeremiah 7:31, 32:35, Ezekiel 16:20-21). God used Babylon to punish Israel for their disobedience. Many children and youth spent their lives in exile (Daniel 1). Israel suffered the curses of disobedience found in Deuteronomy 28:15-68 for not obeying the directions given in Deuteronomy 6.

Parents today still neglect to teach their children. One study of 8,000 adolescents from eleven different denominations demonstrated that only 10% had regular discussions of faith with their parents. Another 43% reported no type of faith discussion with their parents (Bunge, 2008, p. 349). Similar results will impact this generation without drastic changes made by parents and the Church.

Conclusion

God strategically includes children, particularly those in the 4/14 Window, in His plan for the propagation of the Gospel. When writing about Genesis 1:28, Castleberry (2009) states, "the academic literature of missiology has largely ignored migration as a category for understanding and strategizing for the spread of the Gospel" (p. 1). The word children could easily accompany migration in this statement. As seen in the texts presented from Genesis to Deuteronomy, children play a vital role in the spread of the Gospel as seen by the characteristics mentioned about the 4/14 Window Movement.

Missiological literature, discussion, thinking, and strategizing should increasingly include children. Mission planning and effort should incorporate ministry to and by children. Ministerial training needs to include proper and adequate orientation and preparation for ministry to children and parents. Family ministry, including training and encouragement of fathers and mothers, should be a priority in the modern Church. The role of children in the local church as recipients and also as participants must be examined and increased. Contextualized methods of communication and rites of passage need to be developed in local congregations.

Parents, particularly fathers, must intentionally instruct their children to know the Lord. First, they need to develop their own love for the Lord with all their heart and soul and might. Their children need to observe that relationship in the daily life and activities of the parents and the family. Parents need to speak of the Lord, as instructed in Deuteronomy 6, at appropriate times throughout the day. Parents could even use different tools such as a *mezuzah*, some sort of remembrance stones, and rituals that would speak to their children and cause them to ask questions of the faith. Creativity, family dynamics, and children's ages determine the different methods and tools used.

Moses, in his final words said, "Take to heart all the words by which I am warning you today, that you may command them to your children, that they may be careful to do all the words of this law" (Deuteronomy 32:46, ESV). He wanted adults to take to heart the words of the Lord so they could be taught to the children, because through them they would live on in the land the Lord gave them as His chosen people.

Children between the ages of four and fourteen represent a demographic window of opportunity for the Church. Studies show that children in this age group respond in greater numbers than youth and adults. The 4/14 Window promotes a holistic approach to minister to children and involve them in the Kingdom of God.

Deuteronomy 6 includes the *Shema*, which declares the Lord as worthy of complete devotion. Because of His relationship with Israel, His ways and commands demand sharing with the children, the next generation. Parents instruct children in love for the Lord and obedience to His commands so they may live a long life and that it go well with them.

God's intention throughout history as seen in the Old Testament was for parents to speak and model a life dedicated to Him. From Genesis to Deuteronomy, God instructed the patriarchs to be fruitful and multiply implying, as well, instruction of the Lord and His ways. Parents prove key to the passing on of the faith to their children.

In Deuteronomy 6, Moses calls the people of Israel to love the Lord and to make His ways known to the following generations. Moses encouraged teaching in word and example, with the use of rituals and visuals to train children to love the Lord. The children learned of the Lord from their parents as they lived life together.

Time and time again Israel's parents failed to love the Lord and instruct their children to do the same. Thus the Lord fulfilled the promises of judgment found in other parts of Deuteronomy. Israel suffered greatly by not obeying the instructions given by Moses.

May the Church of today heed the words of Moses in Deuteronomy 6 and dedicate effort, time, and resources to those in the 4/14 Window. May parents love the Lord, live as an example for the next generation, so it may go well with them and their days may be long.

References

Barna, G. (2005). *Transforming children into spiritual champions*. Ventura, CA: Regal.

Brewster, D. (2011). *"Child, church, and mission." A resource book for child development workers*. Colorado Springs, CO: Compassion International.

Bunge, M J. (2008). "Biblical and theological perspectives on children, parents, and best practices' for faith formation: Resources for child, youth, and family ministry today." *Dialog* 47: 348-360 doi: 10.1111/j.1540-6385.2008.00414.x.

Castleberry, J. L. (2009). "Procreation, migration, and dominion in Genesis 1:28 and its missiological importance." A paper presented at the 38th Meeting of the Society for Pentecostal Studies, March 26-28, Eugene, OR.

Christensen, D. L. (2002). *Word biblical commentary: Deuteronomy 1:1—21:9*. Nashville, TN: Thomas Nelson.

Edersheim, A. (n.d.). *Sketches of Jewish social life*. E-sword HD Electronic Bible.

Gill, J. (n.d.). *John Gill's exposition of the Bible*. E-sword HD Electronic Bible.

Gonzales, M. P. "The emerging story of the 4/14 movement." http://www.openthe414window.com/history.asp (accessed July 17, 2014).

Hall, G. H. (2000). *Deuteronomy*. Joplin, MO: College Press.

Henry, Matthew. (n.d.). *Matthew Henry's commentary on the whole Bible*. E-sword HD Electronic Bible.

Jamieson, Fausset, and Brown. Jamieson A. R. (n.d.). *Fausset and Brown commentary*. E-sword HD Electronic Bible.

Keil, K. F., & Delitzsch, F. (n.d.). *Keil and Delitzsch commentary on the Old Testament*. E-sword HD Electronic Bible.

McIntosh, D., & Anders, M. E. (2002). *Deuteronomy*. Nashville, TN: Broadman & Holman.

Miller, P. D. (1990). *Deuteronomy*. Louisville, KY: Westminster John Knox Press.

Oberst, B. (1968). *Deuteronomy*. Bible Study Textbook Series. Joplin, MO: College Press.

"What is the 4/14 Window?" http://www.4to14window.com/about/overview (accessed July 17, 2014).

Wright, C. J. H. (2006). *The mission of God: Unlocking the Bible's grand narrative*. Downers Grove, IL: IVP Academic.

Author Biography

Steven R. Entsminger is a missionary with the Assemblies of God World Missions in Spain. Steven is also currently a doctoral student at the Assemblies of God Theological Seminary.

Learning Parenting Skills Through Discipleship

Mike Parrott

It should not be a surprise that parenting terms and skills are used to describe the discipleship process in Scripture. After all, the church is a family. There is a close relationship between what it takes to be a healthy physical family as well as a healthy spiritual family. God even presents Himself in the book of Proverbs as the "pattern for parenting" (Estes, 2005, p. 225). Jesus used parenting terms to describe spiritual family relationships in Luke 8:21 saying, "My mother and my brothers are these who hear the word of God and do it" (New American Standard Bible, NASB). Paul used parenting skills to describe his discipleship role as a "nursing mother" and as a "father" who exhorts, encourages, and implores his own physical children in 1 Thessalonians 2:7 and 11. He also cites the parenting role of a "household manager" as a qualification for local church leadership in 1 Timothy 3:4-5. His own discipleship of Timothy is explained in parenting terms calling Timothy his "true child" (1 Timothy 1:2) and stating that Timothy served Paul like a "child his own father" (Philippians 2:22). John uses parenting terms like father, children, brother, beloved, and fellowship sixty times in 1 John (Cook, 1979, p. 126 footnote). And in 1 John 2:12-14, he describes the stages of discipleship: Little Children for a New Disciple; Children for a Growing Disciple; Young Men for Mature Disciples; and Fathers for Multiplying Disciples (Cook, 1979, p. 116; Parrott, 2010, pp. 72-75).

Through reverse designing the discipleship process—beginning with the end in mind—the skills that are foundational to parenting can be identified, explained, developed, and applied to the parenting process. In this article five critical skills will be addressed: vision casting, modeling, praying, communicating, and leading.

Vision Casting

From the very start of the discipleship process Jesus communicates vision to those He calls. When Jesus comes upon Peter and his brother Andrew casting a net into the sea, He uses terms specific to their fishing passion to get their attention and cast vision saying, "Follow Me, and I will make you fishers of men" (Matthew 4:19; Mark 1:17, NASB). Jesus even communicates the vision personally to Peter saying, "Do not fear, from now on you will be catching men" (Luke 5:10, NASB).

Casting vision involves a plan for reaching the desired ends—Follow Me. It means that the desired end is known—fishers of men or catching men. It also takes into consideration the interests, talents, or skills of the one being challenged—use of the "catching" or "fishing" metaphor of a fisherman. Finally, it involves a specific challenge. Vision casting is not to an event, a meeting, or a job (Hull, 2004, p. 84). It is not "terminal thinking"—viewing "activity and knowledge as an end within themselves" (Hartman & Sutherland, 1976, p. 31). It is a relational thinking process where activities (Follow Me) and knowledge (what one learns from Jesus) lead to a worthwhile and valuable objective (fishing for men or catching men). Jesus makes it clear that through the process of following Him the goal will be reached.

An often used passage to support this skill is Proverbs 29:18, which says, "Where there is no vision, the people are unrestrained, but happy is he who keeps the law" (NASB). First, notice the structure of this text. There is an antithetical parallelism here using the term "but" to contrast the first line with the second one. The text begins with "no vision" and ends with "the law." In the middle the terms "unrestrained" and "happy" are found. The term for "vision" here refers to revelation—truth—God's Word. The English Standard Version (ESV) translates this as "prophetic vision." Both terms "vision" and "law" are referring to God's Word—what He wills. The contrast is between those who have a word from God and those who do not. Estes (2005, p. 225) categorizes this verse under cheerfulness noting "obedience to God's law brings happiness, but those who abandon God's revelation experience disaster." This sounds like what is found in Psalm 1 where the person is delighted to meditate on God's Word day and night. According to Psalm 1:3, the impact of this upon one's life is stability, growth, and success in whatever one pursues. God's Word—His revelation—is the key to vision casting.

Vision casting can be defined as communicating what is on the heart of God in the context of the person's interests so God's purpose is embraced and pursued in His power by faith because one's heart has been captured by it. Notice that this does not involve some "imaginative thinking" to come up with the goal, as that is supplied from a careful study of God's Word. But to actually cast God's vision for the life of a disciple or our own child, it will involve a knowledge of people. The skill of vision casting requires us to be first a student of God's Word, and secondly a student of our own children/disciples.

Being a student of God's Word means learning to handle God's Word well. A simple method to begin doing this is to understand how thoughts develop. Once a statement is made there are only three ways to develop it: explain it, prove it, or apply it (Robinson, 2014, pp. 49-66). As you read God's Word try to identify what the author is talking about. This is more than finding the grammatical subject. It is discovering the complete statement the author wants to address. Then look for how the author develops his statement. What is the author saying about his statement? Does he explain it by saying what it means? Does he advance the argument by proving the statement is true? Or, does he apply it by showing how to do it or what difference it makes? As you study God's Word, you will see what He desires, and this provides the foundation for casting vision in the lives of others (Lowery & McCallum, 2012, pp. 41-45; Kimmel, 2004, pp. 67-92; Reccord, 2005, pp. 37-46).

Second, become a student of your children/disciples. This can be a daunting task when each of your children have different personalities, interests, talents, and passions. People often ask me, "How did each of your four children end up doing such different things as adults?" They are so different: Missionary; Christian camping and Gap Year Director; Children's Emergency Room nurse; and E-commerce Director for a music company. It is true all of them have very different interests, talents, and personalities. I could say my wife and I knew our children so well that we imagined possible outcomes for them based on their unique personalities, interests, skills, and desires and then directed them toward those ends. But we could not have envisioned these unique and specific roles for them.

When my youngest daughter was in her senior year of high school she and I went out to lunch together to discuss her future. Her personality is calm, seeks harmony with others, and is very faithful. But one's personality should not determine what one does, it should only be used to say how a person will carry out any given task. One of her interests included the desire to help others. This caught my attention as we are all called to love God and love others (Matthew 22:37-40). Casting vision for her life meant challenging her toward loving others because it had captured her heart. What was important was connecting the loving of others with her desire to help others and encourage her toward a role that allowed her to do this. As we talked she identified nursing as a possible major in college. With that information we could explore how pursuing that could help her reach the goal of loving others.

When the early disciples were called to follow the Lord, Jesus used the four fishermen's desire to catch fish to lead them toward His purpose of making disciples who make disciples—catching men (Matthew 28:16-20). Vision casting for a parent begins with being a student of God's Word, and then a student of one's children, grandchildren, disciples.

Modeling

Jesus' calling of the four fishermen—Peter, Andrew, James, and John (Matthew 4:18-22; Mark 1:16-20) to follow Him expresses the well-known rabbi-disciple relationship (Barna, 2001, p. 17; Coleman, 1992, p. 53; Hodges, 2001, p. 67; Richards & Martin, 1985, p. 219; Wilkins, 1992, p. 40). In both passages the phrase "Follow Me" comes from three Greek words, "δεῦτε ὀπίσω μου." When "δεῦτε ὀπίσω" are coupled together they mean "come after" or "follow" where the term "ὀπίσω" marks who is to be followed as the leader—the great master-teacher, Jesus (Louw & Nida, 1996, p. 469).

Jesus establishes a discipleship relationship with those He calls where they are to follow Him: watch Him, learn from Him, imitate Him, and be like Him. This relational dynamic is to continue with the next generation of disciples who come to faith in Christ after He is gone. Here is the genius of the Great Commission (Matthew 28:16-20). Jesus commissions His followers to make disciples who make disciples of Jesus. These disciples were to be Christians—little Christs—who looked like Jesus and reproduced followers of Christ. The Apostle Paul demonstrates this practice in 1 Corinthians 11:1, "Be imitators of me, just as I also am of Christ" (NASB). Paul often called upon disciples to imitate him or model what he did as well as to follow the model of others who walked like he did, modeling Christ (1 Corinthians 4:16; Philippians 3:17). Even in the Old Testament this modeling concept is demonstrated in the life of Ezra, who set his heart to study God's law, to practice it, and then to teach it to others (Ezra 7:10).

Being a role model is key to discipleship and parenting. George Barna (2003, p. 120) notes that behavioral modeling with one's own children will push a parent to mature in his or her weak areas. There is nothing like seeing your own son or daughter imitate your behavior. It can humble you or thrill you. A number of years ago, I arrived home from work and found myself walking in on the end of an argument between my wife and my seven-year-old son. I only heard the final comments, and then saw and heard my son loudly stomp upstairs to his room. My wife simply said, "You need to talk with him." Unfortunately, I had more to do than talk about this issue. Only one day earlier he had seen his father—great role model that I am—stomp up the stairs after a disagreement with my wife. Before I could deal with the current issue, I had to apologize to him for my past behavior and then correct his. Being a model does not mean you are perfect, but that you still are the model to follow even in addressing failures.

Some years later, after my oldest son finished college, we were discussing why he had started spending daily time with God way back in junior high. He said, "Every morning when I came downstairs to take a shower before school I would always see you sitting in your office with your Bible open talking with God. It just seemed to be important."

Research shows that the strongest modeling influence in the home comes from a father who has a good relationship with his children and is actively involved (Lynn, 1974; McDowell, 2008; Sarkadi, Kristiansson,

Oberklaid, & Bremberg, 2008, pp. 97, 153-158). In the Back to School 1999 (1999, p. 6) report it was found that, "A teen in a household with a fair or poor relationship with their dad is at 62% greater risk than a teen living with a single mom with an excellent relationship with that mom." Also of note is that "Teenagers living in two-parent families who have a troubled relationship with their fathers are at a higher risk for substance abuse than teens in other families" (Back to School 1999, p. 4).

There is a significant influence upon the family when both parents work together as a unit. Surprisingly, a single parent has more influence on his or her family than a home with both parents when neither are involved (McDowell, 2008).

Praying

There is nothing more important to model than spending time with God. As the early disciples watched Jesus make time for God they caught the priority of prayer (Mark 1:35-39; Luke 5:16; 11:1). It was only a matter of time before the disciples would ask Jesus to explain what they saw Him doing. The devotional life of prayer is the only spiritual life skill that the first century disciples ever asked Jesus to teach them (Luke 11:1).

Recent studies have demonstrated the value of engaging in this spiritual life skill for maintaining a vital relationship with God, overcoming obstacles to spiritual growth, moving from a self-focus to an others-focus, and aligning one's life with God's by developing a heart that beats after God's heart (Barna, 2001; Hawkins & Parkinson, 2007, p. 48; Hawkins & Parkinson, 2008, pp. 83-102; Hawkins & Parkinson, 2011, pp. 155, 181; Parrott, 2010). However, before these benefits can be realized the devotional life of prayer needs to be explained so it can be practiced.

Prayer, what it is and how to do it, stands as the focus of the Sermon on the Mount in Matthew 5-7 (Keener, 2009, p. 206; Nygaard, 2012, p. 30). Lanier (1992, p. 61) notes, "the Lord›s prayer presents not only a model prayer, but a summary of Jesus' priorities embodied in a pattern for all true prayer." Since Tertullian—the first extant commentary on this prayer—it has been understood as two sets of three petitions or six petitions with the first set relating to God and the second set relating to man

(Keener, 2009, pp. 218-221; Calvin, 1975, p. 898; Stevenson, 2004, pp. 3, 28-32, 222). Martin (2015) says, "Lord's Prayer displays a highly poetic form characterized by the recurring use throughout of multiple coordinated figures of speech and thought" (p. 371). When two tri-cola—two sets of three petitions where each set of three is one tri-cola—are found together it is not uncommon to find a relationship between the two sets of petitions (Stocks, 2012, p. 81). Martin (2015, p. 370) notes that the second tri-cola "mirrors" the first tri-cola. Others have applied this to the Disciple's Prayer suggesting an A,B,C//A'B'C' relationship (Day, 2009, p. 27; Parrott, 2010, pp. 40-45; Stevenson, 2000, p. 36).

These insights into this prayer are important to our understanding of it because, "Appreciation of poetic technique can provide crucial clues to the correct interpretation of passages in verse" (Watson, 1994, p. 18). A. Berkeley Mickelsen (1963, p. 44) agrees noting that, "The literary form by which a writer conveys his ideas influences the meaning that they have upon a reader. If we ignore the form, we cannot accurately understand the meaning." The structure of Matthew 6:9-13—two parallel tri-colas forming an A,B,C//A'B'C' pattern—is pictured here in Figure 1. The increasing size of the double arrow in the diagram suggests a synthetic development from line to line (Meynet, 1998, pp. 224-229).

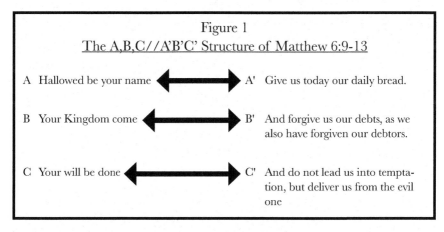

Figure 1
The A,B,C//A'B'C' Structure of Matthew 6:9-13

A Hallowed be your name ⟷ A' Give us today our daily bread.

B Your Kingdom come ⟷ B' And forgive us our debts, as we also have forgiven our debtors.

C Your will be done ⟷ C' And do not lead us into temptation, but deliver us from the evil one

What we discover is that prayer actually defines what the devotional life intends to promote and accomplish in the life of a believer. It begins in a private place free of distractions (Matthew 6:6). It is the cry of a loving relationship between God and a believer that is prompted by the work of the Holy Spirit crying "Abba, Father" (Galatians 4:6). The Holy Spirit Himself, in residence in the disciple (believer), draws him or her into relationship and communication with God for God—note it is the Holy Spirit that prompts the start of the devotional life.

As a believer addresses God as Father, he or she then focuses upon God and His purposes by reading His Word and telling God who He is and what He does (Honoring His Name), discovering what His kingdom is like and desiring it to come (Your Kingdom Come), and discovering God's will and wanting it to be done (Your Will Be Done). Finally, what a believer needs in order to accomplish all of this is addressed: physical provisions, forgiveness, and deliverance from the flesh and the devil.

In teaching prayer, the connections between God and His purposes need to be explained in relationship to what man needs to follow Him (Figure 2). In other words, trusting God for who He is leads to resting in His provisions for our physical bodies. Confessing where we do not measure up to His Kingdom standards provides forgiveness from Him along with the need for forgiveness among one another in the Kingdom community. Dependence upon the power of the

Spirit to do God's will and overcome all obstacles is the final step (cf. Ephesians 5:15-21).

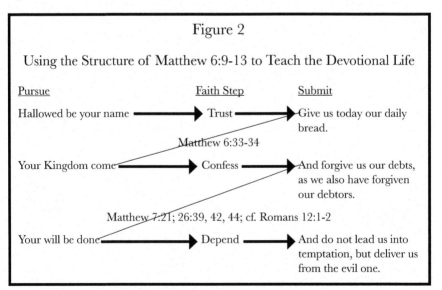

Figure 2

Using the Structure of Matthew 6:9-13 to Teach the Devotional Life

Therefore, the provisions of physical resources, forgiveness, and deliverance are for the purpose of faithfully pursuing God's name, reign, and will on earth here and now. It is in the midst of this pursuit of God and His will that the believer needs physical resources, forgiveness, and deliverance only God supplies. Here is the very heart of prayer—to align the believer's heart with God's heart so he or she will passionately pursue it using His resources.

Time with God also involves intercession. The use of the plurals throughout this model prayer in Matthew: "Our Father," "Give us," "Forgive us," Lead us," and "Deliver us," show the heart of a true member of God's family. They desire for others what they themselves need and seek while on earth, in service and on mission for Him. While it is not wrong to use this model prayer in a corporate manner, the use of the plural phrases refer not to repeating this prayer corporately, but within the context of the setting for this passage—a private place between God and a believer. Each believer must be aware of others, their needs, and ask God to work in their lives too. A practical course of action would be to pray for others about the very same things that he or she has personally discovered from God's Word like Daniel did in Daniel 9. Here Daniel was spending time in Jeremiah the prophet—most likely Jeremiah 29 since that was a letter specifically written to those in Babylon—and noticed in Jeremiah 29:10-11 that the time of their captivity was nearly finished. With this insight from God's Word, Daniel prays for the people and asks God to fulfill His Word. Intercessory prayer was also modeled by Jesus in John 17 and by Paul (Carson, 1992). It would be wise to use these biblical prayers in praying for our children and those we disciple.

By teaching prayer as the devotional life and encouraging its practice, there will be measurable transformation in a believer's convictions, character, and conduct (Parrott, 2010, pp. 125-150). It can be easily taught on a daily basis through a forty-day devotional on devotions (Parrott, 2010, pp. 170-264).

Prayer brings us into communication with God through His Word. Developing a healthy relationship depends upon good communication.

Communicating

There is an expectation of relationship development through communication in the discipleship process. The apostle John was not content to just communicate through "pen and ink," but sought to "speak face to face" with others (2 John 12; 3 John 13-14). In the same way, the apostle Paul aimed toward personal contact with believers to help them grow (Romans 1:9-13; 15:22-24, 28-31). If Paul could not come right away, he would send someone who could represent him like Timothy or Epaphroditus (Philippians 2:19-30). Also, if Paul could not stay as long as needed, he would commission others to remain and complete what was still needed (1 Timothy 1:3; Titus 1:5).

Using pen and ink or modern technology such as e-mail, text messaging, or Instagram are great ways to expose others to truth but it has its limitations. Communication is only 7 percent words but it is 93 percent tone of voice and body language. Unless we are speaking face to face with others or using Skype, FaceTime, or Hangouts in Google we could miss 93 percent of what is being communicated (Tardanico, 2012).

Communication is critical to relationship development. Relationships develop as they move from cliché communication to facts, from facts to opinions, from opinions to feelings, and from feelings to transparency. It used to be that people only shared more openly with those they trusted. However, today there is a loneliness epidemic that is changing this. Communications professor Kory Floyd (2015, p. 9) says that 28 percent of Americans are living alone, one in four have no one with whom to discuss serious matters, and that loneliness has increased among adults by 15 percent in the last decade. Rebecca Foster (2015) comments on Floyd's findings stating, "Ironically, social media and cell phones have made us less close because 'we end up glorifying the trivial … while barely noticing that the substantive and meaningful are missing.'"

Loneliness is also an issue among the Millennial Generation (those born between about 1980 and 2000) and the upcoming Generation Z (born between about 2001 and 2020). Andy Braner (2012, Introduction, para. 2) says that the biggest issue among our youth is that they live alone. He notes that, "even the most popular kids in the school are finding it harder and harder to connect with friends" (Chapter 1, para. 10).

Nearly every student in my classes can identify someone whom they have had only cliché conversations with for all four years of high school or all four plus years of college. Each semester, I ask my college students how many have experienced one of these "four year cliché" relationships suddenly jump all the communication levels to transparency. Surprisingly, there are more and more students experiencing this communication jump each semester. There is a desperate need for real authentic face to face relationships among today's youth and adults. Just look around at those taking their son and/or daughter out for a meal next time you are at a restaurant. How many are actually talking? How many are only eating and using their technology? There is a loneliness epidemic in our land and world today and putting down our technology would be a wise first step (Gil, 2014).

Leading

Parenting terms also describe how Paul related to and led the believers in Thessalonica. He identifies himself in the role of a mother—tenderly caring for her children (1 Thessalonians 2:7). Then he notes the role of a father—one who exhorts, encourages, and implores his children (1 Thessalonians 2:11). The concept of leading a family is a requirement for church leadership where the father "manages his own household well, keeping his children under control with all dignity" (1 Timothy 3:4, NASB) to be an elder or to be "good managers of their children and their own households" to be a deacon. This term "manage" simply means to lead or to care for another. In a Jewish home "the obligation to train the child rested primarily upon the father" (Edersheim, 1979, p. 112). But when the father was not involved in doing this, it could be done by the mother or grandmother. This is seen in the life of Timothy where his father, a Greek—not a believer or God-fearer—was not involved in disciplining and instructing Timothy in the ways of the Lord, but both his mother Eunice and grandmother Lois fulfilled this role (1 Timothy 1:5; 3:14-15; Edersheim, 1979, pp. 115-117).

A new disciple needs nurturing like Paul gave to the Thessalonians. During the first 18 months of physical life, a parent's role is focused on being a nurturer. By the time a child begins to talk—reaches the age where a father can do what Paul did with the Thessalonians: exhort, encourage, and implore—it is time to add the role of Modeler. But what happens after this?

In New Testament times a child reached adulthood at 12 for a woman and 13 for a man. It was expected that a man would marry by 16 or 17, but not later than 20 (Edersheim, 1979, p. 147). Before there was a "youth culture" children moved directly into adulthood. Since WW2 (World War 2), there has been a delay in reaching adulthood that has given rise to a youth culture that is now present in every society in the world. This "delay" has now expanded from puberty to the late twenties (Smith, 2009, p. 6). During this time, parents need to assume the role of a coach.

Coaching or the equipping role is what Paul took on with Timothy when he recruited Timothy as his understudy during Paul's second missionary journey (Acts 16:1-5). It is the training phase of life for teenagers and "emerging adults" (Smith, 2009). The leading skill requires us to adjust our roles along the way from Nurturer to Modeler to Coach and to Peer.

Conclusion

While the Scriptures bring parenting skills to the discipleship process, it is possible to back learn parenting skills through discipleship. Before having children of my own, both my wife and I spent about twelve years in full-time ministry discipling teenagers. These were invaluable years for learning parenting skills. Every skill mentioned above became something we needed to identify, explain, develop, and then apply to the discipling of others. When our own children began arriving we were able to refine what we had learned and improve our own parenting as well as our discipling of others. Learning parenting skills through discipleship helps disciples become great parents as well as effective disciplers. Although the five skills above are just the tip of the parenting and discipling iceberg, they should not be developed all at once. Work on one at a time. Begin with your personal walk with God—your prayer life. Then move to modeling, communicating, vision casting, and leading. What we need today are disciplers who are skilled in parenting and parents who are skilled in discipleship.

This journey will take time and discipline, but it will be well worth the effort and time, so enjoy the journey.

References

Back to School 1999—National survey of American attitudes on substance abuse V: Teens and their parents. (1999). The National Center on Addiction and Substance Abuse (CASA). Retrieved on May 25, 2015 from http://www.casacolumbia.org/addiction-research/reports/survey-american-attitudes-substance-abuse-1999.

Barna, G. (2001). *Growing true disciples*. Colorado Springs, CO: WaterBrook Press.

Barna, G. (2003). *Transforming children into spiritual champions*. Grand Rapids, MI: Baker Books.

Braner, A. (2012). Alone. Colorado Springs, CO: NavPress.

Calvin, J. (1975). *Institutes of the Christian religion, Vol. 2*. John T. McNeill (Ed.). Philadelphia, PA: Westminster Press.

Coleman, R. E. (1992). *The great commission lifestyle*. Grand Rapids, MI: Revell.

Cook, W. R. (1979). *The theology of John*. Chicago, IL: Moody Press.

Day, C. (2009). *The Lord's prayer: A Hebrew reconstruction based on Hebrew prayers found in the Synagogue; Conspectus, Vol. 7*. South African Theological Seminary.

Edersheim, A. (1979). *Sketches of Jewish social life*. Grand Rapids, MI: Eerdmans.

Estes, D. J. (2005). *Handbook on the wisdom books and Psalms*. Grand Rapids, MI: Baker Academic.

Floyd, K. (2015). *The loneliness cure: Six strategies for finding real connections in your life*. Avon, MA: Adams Media.

Foster, R. (2015). The loneliness cure: Six strategies for finding real connections in your life. *ForeWord Reviews*, 10992642, Summer2015, Vol. 18, Issue 3.

Gil, N. (2014). Loneliness: a silent plague that is hurting young people most. *The Guardian*. Retrieved May 25, 2015 from http://www.the-guardian.com/lifeandstyle/2014/jul/20/loneliness-britains-silent-plague-hurts-young-people-most

Hartman, D., & Sutherland, D. (1976). *A guide-book to discipleship*. Eugene, OR: Harvest House.

Hawkins, G. L., & Parkinson, C. (2007). *Reveal: Where are you?* Barrington, IL: Willow Creek.

Hawkins, G. L., & Parkinson, C. (2008). *Follow Me: What's next for you?* Barrington, IL: Willow Creek.

Hawkins, G. L., & Parkinson, C. (2011). *Move: What 1,000 churches real about spiritual growth*. Barrington, IL: Willow Creek.

Hodges, H. (2001). *Tally ho the fox*. Germantown, TN: Spiritual Life Ministries.

Hull, B. (2004). *Jesus Christ disciplemaker*. Grand Rapids, MI: Baker.

Kimmel, T. (2004). *Grace-based parenting*. Nashville, TN: Thomas Nelson.

Keener, C. S. (2009). *The Gospel of Matthew: A socio-rhetorical commentary*. Grand Rapids, MI: Eerdmans.

Lanier, D. E. (1992). The Lord's prayer: Matt 6:9-13—A thematic and semantic-structural analysis. *Criswell Theological Review 6.1*. Wake Forest, NC: Southeastern Baptist Theological Seminary.

Louw, J. P., & Nida, E. A. (1996). *Greek-English lexicon of the New Testament: Based on semantic domains (Vol. 1)*. New York, NY: United Bible Societies.

Lynn, David (1974). *The father: His role in child development*. Monterey, CA: Brooks/Cole.

Martin, M. W. (2015). The poetry of the Lord's prayer: A study in poetic device. *Journal of Biblical Literature*. 134(2), 347–372. doi: http://dx.doi.org/10.15699/jbl.1342.2015.2804

McCallum, D., & Lowery, J. (2012). *Organic discipleship*. Columbus, OH: New Paradigm.

McDowell, J. (2008). *The father connection*. Nashville, TN: B&H.

Meynet, R. (1998). 1998 Rhetorical Analysis: An introduction to biblical rhetoric. *JSOT Sup 256*. Sheffield, UK: Sheffield Academic Press.

Mickelsen, A. B. (1963). *Interpreting the Bible*. Grand Rapids, MI: Eerdmans.

Nygaard, M. (2012). Prayer in the Gospels: A theological exegesis of the ideal prayer. *Biblical Interpretation Series*. Vol 114. Anderson, P. & Sherwood, Y. (Ed.). Leiden; Boston, MA: Brill.

Parrott, M. (2010). His heart, my heart: The role of the devotional life in the discipleship process. (Unpublished doctoral dissertation). Gordon-Conwell Theological Seminary, Charlotte, NC:

Reccord, B., & Reccord, C. (2005). *Launching your kids for life*. Nashville, TN: Word Publishing Group.

Richards, L. O., & Martin, G. (1985). *A theology of personal ministry*. Grand Rapids, MI: Zondervan.

Robinson, H. W. (2014). *Biblical preaching: The development and delivery of expository messages*. Grand Rapids, MI: Baker Academic.

Sarkadi, A., Kristiansson, R., Oberklaid, F., & Bremberg, S. (2008). *Fathers' involvement and children's developmental outcomes: a systematic review of longitudinal studies*. Acta Pædiatrica.

Smith, C. (2009). *Souls in transition*. New York, NY: Oxford University.

Stevenson, K. W. (2000). *Abba Father—Understanding and using the Lord's Prayer*. Harrisburg, PA: Morehouse Publishing.

Stevenson, K. W. (2004). *The Lord's Prayer*. Minneapolis, MN: Fortress Press.

Stocks, S. P. The function of the tricolon in the Psalms of Ascents. Retrieved on October 9, 2014 from https://www.escholar.manchester.ac.uk/api/datastream?publicationPid=uk-ac-man-scw:119691&datastreamId=FULL-TEXT.PDF.

Tardanico, S. (2012). Is social media sabotaging real communication? *Forbes/Leadership*. Retrieved May 25, 2015 from http://www.forbes.com/sites/susantardanico/2012/04/30/is-social-media-sabotaging-real-communication/.

Watson, W. G. E. (1994). *Traditional techniques in classical Hebrew verse*. Sheffield, UK: Sheffield Academic Press.

Wilkins, M. J. (1992). *Following the Master—A biblical theology of discipleship*. Grand Rapids, MI: Zondervan.

Author Biography

Dr. Mike Parrott is the Assistant Professor of Educational Ministries and Assistant Professor of Bible at Cedarville University in Cedarville, Ohio.

Family Ministry in the Midst of a Cataclysmic Cultural Shift in Sexuality

Steve Vandegriff

Abstract: It appears that one does not have to look very far, when it comes to issues that families are facing, especially when those issues go completely contrary to the faith that we desire to instill in our families. There are an ample number of issues that our current culture is pressing forward, with both enthusiasm and public support, that will have impact on what we do with family ministry and how we do family ministry. While there could be some debate as to what those issues are, this article will take a glance at one of the most prominent issues, the homosexual question among biblical passages, and extrapolate pragmatic suggestions. This writer will avoid any proof texting and strive to let the Scriptures speak for itself, and where the Scriptures are silent, will offer macro level insights that should be considered when it comes to family ministry.

Relevant Biblical Passages

Dr. John J. McNeill (1976) (author, war veteran, POW, Jesuit Priest, and psychotherapist) has written several books on the subject of homosexuality and claims, "nowhere in the Scripture is there a clear condemnation of a loving sexual relationship between two gay persons" as described in Feinburg's *Ethics for a Brave New World* (Feinburg, Feinburg, & Huxley, 1993, p. 311). While condemnation might be a strong term, the Scriptures do give us clear guidelines on this cultural and moral issue. The following are the scriptural passages that bring up this issue of homosexuality.

Genesis 19:1–11

The biblical story of Sodom and Gomorrah is an enduring description of a society at its lowest moral level. The traditional explanation of Sodom and Gomorrah's demise has been directly related to the sinful lifestyle of practicing "sodomy" or homosexual behavior on a grand scale. Homosexuals have challenged this interpretation in two ways: Firstly, they argue it was not homosexuality that was the tipping point for God. It was homosexual rape. This sin was the victimization of the non-consenting individual. This would suggest that the text is silent on homosexual behavior as long as the two parties mutually consent. Secondly, the corporate sin of Sodom and Gomorrah was not homosexuality, but an extreme lack of hospitality (this is certainly a more outrageous interpretation of Genesis 19). This interpretation centers on the phrase, "to know." Obviously, the thought process here is that "to know" has no sexual connotation. John Feinberg addresses that interpretation this way:

> The sexual understanding of yāda' in Gen 19:5 is supported by its use in the immediate context of the Sodom story (v. 8). In verse 8 the same verb has to mean "to have sexual relations with," for it makes no sense to say Lot's daughters were not acquainted with any men. If nothing else, they knew Lot, and he was surely a man! Even Bailey's claim that Lot's offer of his daughters was just the most attractive bribe available does not avoid the sexual use of the verb. He was offering his daughters for sexual use to the men of the city. The verb in verse 8 clearly has a sexual meaning (Feinberg, et al., 1993, p. 314).

From a more colloquial explanation, if the men of Sodom wanted to be more hospitable and collegial then Lot could have simply introduced everyone. But the narrative and context of this story is clear that a crowd of men were overtaken by the prospect of new sexual partners with an unbridled sexual appetite that was facilitated by a culture that had no moral restraints. It appears that this group of men could not even be distracted from homosexual sex by heterosexual sex, indicating the possibility of being unsatisfied or bored with heterosexual sex. (While this is more anecdotal on this writer's perspective, there have been individuals (on the relatives' side and on the friends' side) who have trudged into a progression (or digression) of homosexual behavior simply due to a boredom in heterosexual behavior, possibly seeking a new sexual experience that would bring a more stimulating or heightened sensation.)

The book of Jude (verse 7) gets into the conversation by specifically mentioning Sodom and Gomorrah. Jude gives a clear commentary on the sin of Sodom. These unnatural sex acts are described as pursuing an "unnatural desire" (English Standard Version, ESV). The strong language used by Jude indicates that the inhabitants of Sodom and Gomorrah were completely obsessed with their sexually immoral behavior.

Leviticus 18:22 and 20:13

Moving to Leviticus we find verses directed toward the people of Israel. Leviticus 18:22 and 20:13 deal with the topic of homosexuality. All of the Leviticus exhortations are intended to set Israel apart from their neighbors who did not follow the true God of Israel, and were known for idol worship and immorality. Some who embrace homosexual behavior claim that homosexuality is condemned in these verses because it was practiced in conjunction with idolatry and pagan rituals, not because it is inherently wrong. However, Feinberg et al. (1993) points out:

The Leviticus texts just naturally assume the practices are condemned because they are inherently wrong, not because they were part of the idolatrous worship of the Egyptians and Canaanites. In the Leviticus Code incest, adultery, child sacrifice, bestiality, spiritism and the cursing of one's parents are all prohibited. Only one act condemned in the Code has cultic or symbolic significance—child sacrifice, and it is condemned whether associated with religious worship or not. Child sacrifice was practiced in pagan religious rites, but it was wrong on two counts—in itself and because of its association with idolatry. As a matter of fact, that the surrounding nations practiced both child sacrifice and the other prohibited acts only serves to confirm the corruption of these cultures in the mind of the Israelite. Moreover, homosexuality is condemned in the context of adultery, bestiality, and incest. Clearly, those practices were not prohibited simply because of their association with idolatry or Egyptian and Canaanite culture (p. 328).

Probably the more popular opinion about this Leviticus passage(s) is that anything to do with the Mosaic Law is of minimal importance, and some parts are irrelevant in the 21st century. This view argues that the Mosaic Law has no relevance for us today. Romans 10:4, "For Christ is the end of the law for righteousness to everyone who believes" (ESV), along with Hebrews 7:11, is used to say that Christ ended the Law. Juxtaposed with this interpretation, is a perception that there is a distinct line between the moral and ceremonial elements of the law. While the moral elements are still obligatory, the ceremonial aspects of the law are antiquated and non-compulsory. This applies to any prohibitions against homosexuality as well, since it is part of these ceremonial instructions. While there is an element of truth here (enjoy a rare steak as opposed to Leviticus 17:10), when it comes to disregarding certain ceremonial instructions, it would be foolish to disregard *any* biblical instructions especially those that are repeated in the New Testament. Along with consideration of the moral and ethical absolutes behind the ceremonial instructions, they simply make sense and have benefits for compliance as well as consequences for defiance, both personally and corporately. There should also be consideration of the categorical implications. Categories of diet certainly have less consequential implications than sexual behavior, and sexual behavior involves more than one person (not to mention the intertwined relationships who have emotional connections).

Romans 1:26–27

This passage could be the clearest warning when it comes to homosexuality. This passage deals with lesbianism while 1:27 treats male homosexuality. The main misinterpretation of this passage is that Paul is condemning unnatural homosexual actions, not homosexuality or the homosexual, or even "responsible" homosexual behavior. In other words, Paul is speaking against heterosexual individuals who are committing homosexual acts. This explanation is a good example of faulty reasoning, reducing homosexuality to nothing more than a variation of nature just like a person who happens to be short, tall, or has freckles. It appears here that homosexual behaviorists are making homosexuality a genetic or innate condition, which is still up for debate. The argument continues to be pressed that going against nature is referring to homosexual acts by heterosexuals or heterosexual acts by homosexuals thus acting against one's natural inclinations, with no fear of physical, emotional, or spiritual consequences. This writer asserts that this passage is clear that homosexual behavior is against the sexuality that is established in nature. On a more lay level, the conventional wisdom has been that homosexual behavior simply does not make sense and one does not have to go any further than the animal world, to see that. This train of thought is supported in Scripture:

> 58.9 φυσικός, ή, όν; φυσικῶς: pertaining to that which is in accordance with the nature or character of something—'natural, naturally, by nature, by instinct.'
>
> φυσικός: μετήλλαξαν τὴν φυσικὴν χρῆσιν εἰς τὴν παρὰ φύσιν 'they changed the use which is in accordance with nature to that which is contrary to nature' Ro 1:26. For some languages the equivalent of 'being in accordance with nature' is simply 'being as it should be.' ζῷα γεγεννημένα φυσικὰ εἰς ἅλωσιν καὶ φθοράν 'natural creatures born to be caught and killed' 2 Peter 2:12. In place of an expression such as 'natural creatures' a more appropriate equivalent in some languages is simply 'animals.'
>
> φυσικῶς: ὅσα δὲ φυσικῶς ὡς τὰ ἄλογα ζῷα ἐπίστανται 'which they know by instinct, like wild animals' Jude 10 (Louw & Nida, 1989, p. 1.118).

Another attempt to discredit Paul's teaching is to equivocate this admonition to the Apostle Paul simply stating his opinion, which he has done in previous passages (e.g. 1 Corinthians 7:40). As a result, we can accept or reject them. Yet if one carefully looks at Paul's instructions on homosexuality, he never states that he is expressing his personal opinions and he is also reflecting what is stated in the Old Testament.

A final argument focuses on the word "lust" in Romans 1:27. Here the emphasis is on the (wrong) motive of homosexual behavior, that being of lust. In essence, lust is wrong but homosexuality is not, especially if homosexuality is based upon love and commitment. A parallel of this rationale could be compared to an old adage of one being sincere but sincerely wrong. James 1:15 states, "Then desire [lust] when it has conceived gives birth to sin, and sin when it is fully grown brings forth death" (ESV). Desire (lust) is always a precursor and applies to both homosexual and heterosexual activity, but to justify homosexuality out of sincere motives simply ignores what Scripture is clearly saying.

1 Corinthians 6:9–11 and 1 Timothy 1:8–10

These passages contain a list of wrong behaviors that incudes Greek words related to this topic. Holman's Illustrated Bible explains:

> In 1 Tim. 1:8–10 Paul discusses the value of the OT law in the present era, if used wisely. It is to be used to judge "sinners." Then he includes "homosexuals" (arsenokoitai) in his vice list, which delineates those who are "the ungodly." Also in 1 Cor. 6:9–11 "homosexuals" appears in a similar vice list, and Paul comments that anyone who continues in these sins will not inherit the kingdom of God. Arsenokoites refers to the active partner in the homosexual act. However, in addition to "homosexuals" in 1 Cor. 6:9, Paul adds a second word, "effeminate" (malakoi). Malakoi refers to the passive member in the homosexual relationship (Holman, 2006, p. 778).

Whether the actual term "homosexuality" is used or not, is irrelevant. The Greek words clearly describe the behavior, although it is infrequent. This infrequency is probably because many Greeks, engaged in homosexual acts, were often bisexual since many were in a heterosexual marriage relationship. Furthermore, homosexuality was not prevalent in Jewish culture. At first glance, this list appears to show we are all spiritually doomed (which is true if not for the grace of God and the sacrifice of His Son). But this would overlook the distinction between those who repent and those who are unrepentant. Man's choice is clearly in play here.

It should be noted that the ESV uses the phrase, "nor men who *practice* homosexuality." This brings up a controversial matter of being a homosexual and being a practicing homosexual. This writer proposes that there is a difference, when it comes to sinful behavior, and would also suggest that both are redeemable. This would also apply to heterosexuals who remain celibate, versus those who engage in immorality. The attraction part of this spiritual equation is the temptation and Scripture teaches us, "the temptations in your life are no different from what others experience. And God is faithful. He will not allow the temptation to be more than you can stand. When you are tempted, he will show you a way out so that you can endure" (1 Corinthians 10:13, New Living Translation, NLT). "God blesses those who patiently endure testing and temptation. Afterward they will receive the crown of life that God has promised to those who love him" (James 1:12, NLT). James goes on to describe this progression from temptation that is linked to our desires, then from desires to sinful actions, which inevitably leads to death (both physically and spiritually). Romans 6:23 states the inevitable as well as hope that only comes through Christ, "For the wages of sin is death, but the free gift of God is eternal life through Christ Jesus our Lord" (NLT). So while the temptation is not wrong, the acting and yielding to that temptation is not only wrong, but it starts a downward progression that can only be inverted by the acknowledgement and embracing of God's plan for our lives. For the homosexual individual who struggles with these temptations of attraction, Luke 9:23, says "And he said to all, 'If anyone would come after me, let him deny himself and take up his cross daily and follow me'" (ESV). Combine this with 1 Corinthians 10:13 and a community of believers who follow after righteousness (1 Timothy 6:11), and the same-sex attracted individual will be able to take this journey. Holman's provides some inspirational commentary.

> There is the opportunity to be forgiven, changed, and declared righteous through Jesus Christ. Paul continues in 1 Cor. 6:11 (HCSB) to say, "Some of you were like this." The Corinthian church evidently contained some former homosexuals who had been converted. Furthermore, Paul adds of them, "But you were washed, you were sanctified, you were justified in the name of the Lord Jesus Christ and by the Spirit of our God." The homosexual who repents and believes receives the same cleansing, sanctification, and justification as every other believer who turns from sin to Christ (Holman, 2006. p. 778).

Where Do We Go From Here?

In their book, *Ex-Gays? A Longitudinal Study of Religiously Mediated Change in Sexual Orientation*, Stanton Jones and Mark Yarhouse (2007) did a study to determine if change in sexual orientation is possible, via a religious ministry. The other element in this study was to determine if change is possible and if change is harmful. According to the American Psychiatric Association, "There is no published scientific evidence supporting the efficacy of 'reparative therapy' as a treatment to change one's sexual orientation. The potential risks of 'reparative therapy' are great, including depression, anxiety, and self-destruction." The American Psychological Association says that sexual orientation is impossible to change. So the stakes are high on the expectations of this research project. On average, in conjunction with the Exodus Ministry (Exodus International) process revealed statically significant change away from homosexual orientation and toward heterosexual orientation. The change away from homosexual orientation is more significant than the change toward heterosexual orientation. Their results indicate that change is possible for some. It does not indicate that change is possible for everyone. As well, the attempt to change is not dramatically harmful to individuals (Jones & Yarhouse, 2007). In somewhat of a twist, Exodus International unanimously voted to close its doors after decades of helping people overcome homosexual behavior, opting for a new name and new mission (Reduce Fear Ministries).

Russell D. Moore, president of the Ethics & Religious Liberty Commission, said the folding of Exodus International "doesn't mean the folding of an evangelistic sexual ethic, though it does mean a move away from a therapeutic model of sexual sanctification." "Evangelical Christianity increasingly addresses sexual issues more in line with the older Christian tradition of sin and temptation and triumph than with the language of therapy," Moore told Baptist Press. "We can't have a utopian view of overcoming temptation of any sort." Jesus never promises any Christian freedom from temptation, Moore said, but He does promise the power of the Spirit to fight against the pull to temptation, whatever the temptation may be.

"Increasingly churches are addressing persons with same-sex attractions the same way they address everyone else: in terms of the Gospel and a lifelong call to take up one's cross and follow Christ," Moore said. "This means the Christian grappling with same-sex attractions needs to hear that the Gospel addresses him or her, and that this person needs the whole body of Christ, in community, not just an accountability group of those who are defined by the same temptations."

R. Albert Mohler Jr., president of Southern Baptist Theological Seminary, said it became clear last year—when the president, Alan Chambers suggested that people can persist in homosexual behavior and still receive the salvation that Jesus offers—that Chambers and Exodus International were rethinking their understanding of a Christian approach to homosexuality. "Sadly, it appears that this rethinking has resulted in something like a surrender to the cultural currents of the day," Mohler told Baptist Press (Roach, 2013).

The American Psychological Association defines conversion therapy as aimed at changing sexual orientation, but adopted a resolution in 2009 condemning the practice. In its resolution the organization said "mental health professionals should avoid telling clients that they can change their sexual orientation through therapy or other treatments." The same resolution encouraged therapists to consider the religious beliefs of clients who say such beliefs are important to their views of homosexuality (Payne, 2013). According to The Baptist Standard, the American Association of Christian Counselors (50,000 members) amended its code of ethics to eliminate the promotion of reparative therapy and encouraged celibacy instead. Not everyone is in agreement, when it comes to same sex attraction and celibacy. "My conclusion is that if sexual orientation is one's enduring pattern of sexual attraction, then the Bible teaches both same-sex behavior and same-sex orientation to be sinful," Denny Burk, a biblical studies professor at Southern Baptist Theological Seminary, wrote in a blog post for the Southern Baptist Convention's Ethics & Religious Liberty Commission (Bailey, 2014).

It seems that cultural sentiment is favorable to all things homosexual (GLBTQ: Gay, Lesbian, Bisexual, Transgender, and Queer). For those in the faith community, who embrace all things biblical, and specifically those involved in family ministry, there needs to be some clarity and direction. There is no doubt that the Scriptures are clear about homosexuality, not just an indictment but also a protection for individuals and societies, and the most basic institution established in Genesis, being the traditional family. There may never be a consensus on the definition of marriage and family now but that should not silence those of faith. First Peter 3: 1-2 gives an example of a more quiet approach, even in the midst of unbelievers, "Wives, in the same way submit yourselves to your own husbands so that, if any of them do not believe the word, they may be won over without words by the behavior of their wives, when they see the purity and reverence of your lives" (New International Version, NIV). Their voice can be loud by exemplifying what a traditional family looks like and acts like. As people of faith (in Christ), not only is what we say important but also how we say it. First Peter 3:15 says, "But in your hearts revere Christ as Lord. Always be prepared to give an answer to everyone who asks you to give the reason for the hope that you have. But do this with gentleness and respect" (NIV). There also needs to be a sincere desire to minister to homosexuals (GLBTQ) because our theology says that we are to come to Christ just as we are. Change happens afterward (2 Corinthians 5:17). We want to facilitate ministry that nurtures one's search for faith and forgiveness and we welcome anyone who is on this search. When it comes to inquiring young minds (in family ministry), there should be no hesitation about God's love for everyone (John 3:16), and also clarity as to the instructions from Scripture when it comes to a loving and nurturing nuclear family. That standard has to be championed. We also need to know what our lines are…the point where we go no further.

While we wrestle with the sentiments of cultural gyrations about morality, we need to continue the noble task of family ministry. As this conversation continues, it would be beneficial for family ministry to glean from a study that was done by the University of North Carolina among teenagers. This study, named the *National Study of Youth and Religion* (NSYR), was the largest and most detailed such study ever undertaken. The NSYR conducted a nationwide telephone survey of teens and significant caregivers, as well as nearly 300 in-depth face-to-face interviews with a sample population. The results were detailed in the book, *Soul Searching: The Religious and Spiritual Lives of American Teenagers.* There have been authors who have penned books addressing the findings of this book (Dean, 2010) and alongside *Soul Searching,* there were some reoccurring themes that those in family ministry might take notice:

1. Religion is a significant presence in the lives of many teenagers.
2. Contrary to many popular assumptions and stereotypes, the character of teenager religiosity in the U. S. is extraordinarily conventional.
3. The single most important social influence on the religious and spiritual lives of adolescents is their parents.
4. It appears that the greater the supply of religiously grounded relationships, activities, programs, opportunities, and challenges available to teenagers, other things being equal, the more likely teenagers will be religiously engaged.
5. Adolescent religious and spiritual understanding and concern seem to be generally weak. Most U. S. teens have a difficult to impossible time explaining what they believe, what it means, and what the implications of their beliefs are for their lives (Smith & Denton, 2005, pp. 260-263).

The conclusions are obvious and transferable to all aspects of family ministry. Religious congregations that prioritize ministry to youth and support for their parents, invest in trained and skilled youth group leaders, and make serious efforts to engage and teach adolescents seem much more likely to draw youth into their religious lives and foster religious and spiritual maturity in their young members (Smith & Denton, 2005, p. 261).

The Heart of the Matter

The majority of pro-homosexual behavioral arguments totally ignore the inspiration of the Scriptures and the divine source of these commands. These commands are not the result of human speculation and superstition, but are from God and the Scriptures. In the book, *Truth in a Culture of Doubt*, the authors capsulize this dilemma of being told what to do, and particularly being told what to do by an omniscient God. Going contrary to God's direction can be classified as sinful or evil. This can be a difficult concept for people to grasp or admit. I think it would be universally accepted that when people hurt others for no apparent reason, that is evil personified. But the Scriptures go one step further.

> "...this is only part of what makes evil so intolerable. According to the Bible, evil is evil because it offends a holy and righteous God. The magnitude of this offense is difficult for humans to imagine, especially in this day and age when personal accountability is in increasingly short supply. We don't like anyone telling us what to do. But the Bible teaches that, in a general sense, all suffering is rooted in cosmic rebellion against a God who tried to tell us what to do. How dare He? Due to this rebellion, the good and perfect world God created descended in a downward spiral" (Köstenberger, Bock, & Chatraw, 2014, p. 29).

Juxtaposed to this, is the absence of personal responsibility. It is becoming clear that our modern Western culture is more intolerant of anyone or anything that even resembles having an articulate truth that combines divine inspiration and a common sensibility. At times the perception is that those of faith should not speak to cultural issues, but it is clear that the issue of homosexuality was a moral issue long before it became a cultural issue (and cultural issues would be noticeably deficient if they lacked input and wisdom from faith-based individuals).

It should also be noted that just because something is culturally acceptable, does not make it right. While there are three responses to culture, only one is the most constructive. One response is to be offended by what we see or experience with culture and we withdraw (from culture). There is no doubt there are situations where this might be a viable option, but I don't see this as an example emulated in Scripture. Another response is to be happy with what we see in culture and assimilate into culture, almost an acceptance of all things culturally acceptable. A third response is one of being distressed by what we see in culture and as a result become engaged in culture (in our current vernacular—we become part of the conversation). The balancing act is being an unbalanced immersionist who gains an audience but loses his Message. Then there is the unbalanced rejectionist who maintains his Message but loses his audience. The attainable ideal is becoming a balanced communicator who uses critical observation and cultural participation. The Apostle Paul gives a strong example of this in Acts 17:22-23, "So Paul, standing before the council, addressed them as follows: "Men of Athens, I notice that you are very religious in every way, for as I was walking along I saw your many shrines. And one of your altars had this inscription on it: 'To an Unknown God.' This God, whom you worship without knowing, is the one I'm telling you about" (NLT). Also, in 1 Chronicles 12:32, "from Issachar, men who understood the times and knew what Israel should do..." (NIV). We need to be people who understand our times and know what we should do.

Conclusion

While a writer would be wise to avoid sounding too definitive and conclusive on cultural matters, there are places where the Scriptures are both definitive and conclusive. There are also times where the Scriptures are silent. It is the silence of Scripture that drives us to lean on the broader biblical instructions given to us, while incorporating wisdom, good decision-making, common sensibility, and pragmatic function. Regardless whether the Scriptures are crystal clear or not, debate, confusion, and polarization persist on many fronts (issues). Yet in spite of all this conversation, there is a need for those of faith to challenge the cultural lexicon, as well as be part of the conversation, while being a good listener and a good conversationalist.

References

Bailey, S. P. (2014, August 10). Gay, celibate Christians 'easily misunderstood.' *The Baptist Standard.* (August 10, 2014). Retrieved from https://www.baptiststandard.com/news/faith-culture/16805-gay-celibate-christians-easily-misunderstood.

Dean, K. C. (2010). *Almost Christian: What the faith of our teenagers is telling the American church.* New York, NY: Oxford University Press.

Feinberg, J. S., Feinberg, P. D., & Huxley, A. (1993). *Ethics for a brave new world.* Wheaton, IL: Crossway Books.

Jones, S. L., & Yarhouse, M A. (2007). *Ex-gays: A longitudinal study of religiously mediated change in sexual orientation.* Downers Grove, IL: IVP Academic. Retrieved from http://www.ivpress.com/videos/2846.php.

Köstenberger, A. J., Bock, D. L., & Chatraw, J. D. (2014). *Truth in a culture of doubt: Engaging skeptical challenges of the Bible.* Nashville, TN: B & H.

Louw, J. P., & Nida, E. A. (1989). *Greek-English lexicon of the New Testament: Based on semantic domains.* New York, NY: United Bible Societies.

McNeill, J. (1976). *The church and the homosexual.* Boston, MA: Beacon Press. Retrieved from http://www.johnjmcneill.com/TCTH.HTML.

Payne, E. (2013, July 8). *Group apologized to gay community, shuts down 'cure' ministry.* Retrieved from http://www.cnn.com/2013/06/20/us/exodus-international-shutdown/index.html.

Roach, E. (2013, June 20). *Exodus Int'l closes after Chambers' apology.* Irvine, CA: Baptist Press. Retrieved from http://townhall.com/news/religion/2013/06/20/exodus-intl-closes-after-chambers-apology-n1623864.

Smith, C., & Denton, M. L. (2005). *Soul searching: The religious and spiritual lives of American teenagers.* New York, NY: Oxford University Press.

The Holman Illustrated Study Bible. (2006). Nashville, TN: Holman Bible Publishers.

Author Biography

Dr. Steve Vandegriff is the Professor of Christian Leadership and Church Ministries at Liberty University in Lynchburg, Virginia.

The Teaching Mother An Expositional Examination Of "Mother" in Proverbs

Daniel A. Webster

Author Note: All Scripture used is English Standard Version, ESV.

When reading the Proverbs of the Old Testament, it does not take long to notice that an overwhelming majority of these sayings are directed to men for the problems encountered by men. As the reader continues moving through this didactic collection, it becomes evident that the Proverbs are explicitly and implicitly directed at men during an age when instruction was necessary and appropriate for the circumstances of these men (Kroeger & Evans, 2002, p. 320).

Why is this the case? One may conclude that males, being more inclined to foolishness, need more instruction in wisdom and that females are generally wiser individuals. This stands to reason when considering a *woman's intuition* or the *sixth sense,* which was observed by Rudyard Kipling when he said, "a woman's guess is much more accurate than a man's certainty." Could it be that men in general lack discretion and thus need a book of memorable maxims in order to compete in culture?

Another theory may be the male domination of culture. An overview of the Bible reveals a cultural context in the Old Testament with a thriving patriarchal system. The New Testament reveals a system that seems to compliment the Roman *paterfamilias*. References refer to God the *Father,* God the *Son*, and Christ as the believer's *brother*. Furthermore, there are references likening the Christian life to spiritual warfare and sporting events, which were both accomplished by men at the time of the writing. Should woman view the book of Proverbs—and all Scripture for that matter—as another triumph in the conquest of male chauvinism?

Neither inferior intellect nor gender bigotry is the explanation for the matter at hand. In fact, God in no way decrees male *domination* but male *headship* (Ortlund, n.d.) and in doing so established the man as the head of the home and the leaders of His church (Genesis 1:26-28; 1 Timothy 2:12-14, 3:2-12; Ephesians 5:23-25; 1 Corinthians 11:8-9; 1 Peter 3:1-7; 1 Corinthians 14:34-35; Titus 1:5-9). While much could be stated about this God-ordained order, all that will be said is that women should be encouraged in the fact that there is no relation between personal role and personal worth (Ortund). The Proverbs were written in order to steer the lives of young men toward right in an attempt to rescue society, the home, and the collective direction of God's people. Throughout this book, written mainly for men, are beautiful ascriptions to women. More unmistakable are the fifteen references to mothers that provide instruction for the men of Proverbs who may fail with it. An expositional examination of verses specifically mentioning mothers will give appreciation for the role of women as presented in Proverbs. In an anthem sung as tribute to Godly mothers everywhere, Proverbs reinforces the commonly quoted line that states, "The hand that rocks the cradle is the hand that rocks the world."

A Comprehensive Overview

Although this study will focus exclusively on mothers, it is advantageous to note that of the over 900 proverbs, 98 mention women specifically (excluding the personification of wisdom and folly). Table 1 provides an overview and break down of the 15 maternal proverbs and Tables 2-4 give an overview of the 83 remaining references. The verses warning young men of the adulterous women are included since they are constructive, by use of a negative example, in teaching women how to conduct themselves.

The Teaching Mother
Table 1

1.1 *The Mother as Teacher*

1:8 Hear, my son, your father's instruction, and forsake not your mother's teaching.

6:20 My son, keep your father's commandment, and forsake not your mother's teaching.

31:1 The words of King Lemuel. An oracle that his mother taught him.

1.2 *Rejoicing*

10:1 A wise son makes a glad father, but a foolish son is a sorrow to his mother.

15:20 A wise son makes a glad father, but a foolish man despises his mother.

23:25 Let your father and mother be glad; let her who bore you rejoice.

1.3 *Respect*

19:26 He who does violence to his father and chases away his mother is a son who brings shame and reproach.

20:20 If one curses his father or his mother, his lamp will be put out in utter darkness.

23:22 Listen to your father who gave you life, and do not despise your mother when she is old.

28:24 Whoever robs his father or his mother and says, "That is no transgression," is a companion to a man who destroys.

30:11 There are those who curse their fathers and do not bless their mothers.

30:17 The eye that mocks a father and scorns to obey a mother will be picked out by the ravens of the valley and eaten by the vultures.

31:28 Her children rise up and call her blessed; her husband also, and he praises her:

1.4 *Rod and Reproof*

4:3 When I was a son with my father, tender, the only one in the sight of my mother.

29:15 The rod and reproof give wisdom, but a child left to himself brings shame to his mother.

The Fact *That* She Taught
See Table 1.1

The most prominent characteristic of the mother presented in Proverbs is that she is a teacher. Much can be learned by the fact that in Hebrew culture the mother was instrumental in the upbringing of sons. Both 1:8 and 6:20 command the son not to forsake his mother's teaching. The early childhood of peasants and future kings alike were woman-centered (Gammie & Purdue, 1990, p. 161) and the pairing of father and mother in twelve of the fifteen maternal references (as seen in Table 1) reinforce this fact. At first consideration, one may conclude that the mother's inferior teaching needs the backing of the father and so the pairing; but, this is not the case. In fact, the *mother's torah* is just as real and binding as the *father's instruction* (Gammie & Purdue, 1990). What a tribute to Israel's mothers! Furthermore, while it is customary in ancient Near East wisdom literature to address the crown prince, the first section of Proverbs is not addressed to a particular heir thus making Solomon's admonitions in 1:8 and 6:20 for all sons of all times (Longman, 2008, p. 47). The fact that Solomon's readers would have identified with the lessons learned at home from the matriarch further substantiates the reality of her vital and equal role as teacher.

Another reference to the teaching mother is the discourse of wisdom from King Lemuel found in chapter 31, which is an oracle that his mother taught him. This verse is one of the three references that do not pair the mother's teaching with the father's. A mother teaching her son who is soon to be the king is not foreign to ancient literature. This is also found in Egyptian literature (Martin, 1995, p. 78), which predates the Old Testament Proverbs by more than 1,000 years (Whybray, 1994, p. 153). The consideration of this Egyptian context brings to mind the training put in place by Pharaoh's daughter for Moses. By God's sovereignty and providence Jochebed, the birth mother of Moses, would still be able to play a large part in teaching her little boy. To honor Jehovah and his mother, when Moses was grown up, he refused to be called the son of Pharaoh's daughter (Hebrews 11:24). In understanding the maternal role in the Ancient Near East context, it is important to note that Egypt's princess had the privilege and responsibility to appoint who would raise and educate her new son (Exodus 2:1-10). Pharaoh is not consulted in the biblical narrative (neither is Moses' father); the women handled these details. It is not uncommon in ancient civilization to see the mother as a reigning monarch who is instructing the crown prince in the ways of the monarch he would one day obtain (Martin, 1995, p. 79). This is also seen in Babylonian literature, which more closely dates the writings of the Hebrew Proverbs (Whybray, 1994, p. 153).

With these observations in view, we must not forget the role of the father in the Christian home; the father's absenteeism is causing widespread destruction in the home. However, motherhood is in trouble as well. A mother's task is far more than providing a babysitting service—mother's are to *teach*, not merely *keep* their children. Often, newly pregnant young mothers see their unborn baby as a future "pet," which provides an opportunity to post cute pictures on social media sites. (The author is well acquainted with an individual who owns a 4D Ultrasound Studio. This individual has observed this "pet" mentality in many of their young mothers.) Other times, new mothers view their child as an inconvenience—a mere obstruction to the furtherance of a career. The wisdom literature calls mothers to step up... be teachers!

What She Taught
See Table 1.2 and 1.3

The specific lesson taught to King Lemuel by his mother in Proverbs 31:1-9 remained with him his entire life. In verse 2, one is captivated by the love of this mother as she passionately pleas with the "son of my womb" who is the "answer to my prayers." In the following seven verses, "she bids him beware of lust (verse 3) and excess wine (verses 4-7), and urges him to befriend the helpless (verse 8), and to judge righteously (verse 9)" (Perowne, 1899, p. 186). Her petition makes it seem as if "some besetting enticements were imminent, perhaps already working poison in her beloved son" (Bridges, 1959, p. 617). Wild women and excessive wine are not for the serious-minded king, and this mother makes a convincing case for this fact. Instead of "the indulgence of appetite, which will only debase thy nature" the son is challenged to lead a life of self-denial and leave these things alone. No doubt this mother desired her once little boy to stay away from the extremes of alcohol and sexuality to ensure the sound judgment she urges in verses 8-9. Both King Ahasuerus (Esther 1) and King Herod (Matthew 14, Mark 6) made unjust decisions while under the influence of alcohol and sexual excitement (Bridges, 1959, p. 618). A position of power always provides the opportunity to make one above the law. This was the case with Israel's king. While some monarchs have seized the opportunity to pervert justice in favor of the rich and powerful, King Lemuel was challenged to defend the rights of the poor and needy. The king, during this time of history, acted as the supreme judge who reviewed most of the appeals of injustice. This judicial function as seen in Solomon's judgment, which rules in favor of the poor widow (Whybray, 1972, p. 181), was common in this period (1 Kings 3; 2 Samuel 14).

So how can this be applied to a modern context? The king's mother instructed her son to honor Jehovah by contributing positively to society by not taking advantage of his neighbor. This echoes the great commandment to love God and love your neighbor (Matthew 22:36-40). The example set forth by the mothers of Proverbs gives a large task to mothers today. It is the mother's responsibility to impart the Christian virtues taught in God's Word. Not mere external conformity—but actions that show an overflow of the heart. Even in a patriarchal society, these portions of Old Testament wisdom literature place the yoke of spiritual instruction in the home on women as well as men. There is much to be profited in knowing *that* the mother taught and *what* she taught. Even still, *how* she taught can be seen in the text.

How She Taught
See Table 1.2, 1.3, and 1.4

The methods employed by the mother can be clearly seen in four words: rod, reproof, respect, and rejoicing. Proverbs 29:15 states, "The rod and reproof give wisdom, but a child left to himself brings shame to his mother." God ordains the disciplining of adults for government (Romans

13:3-4); however, Proverbs make it clear that parents are to dispense it to their children. The mother's first line of influencing her child unto righteousness is verbal reproof (The Hebrew word for "reproof" has verbal implications. It can also mean "chide" or "argue," which are both verbal means.) and her last resort is corporal punishment. For this reason, there is a very obvious distinction between "the rod" and "reproof" in the text.

"Proverbs is well known for its praise of the rod" (13:24; 23:13-15; 29:15), but the rod is not a cure-all (Kidner, 1975, pp. 50-51). Much reproof should come before the use of physical correction. The Hebrew noun for "reproof" is *towkechah* (Strong's 8433, הַחְכוֹת), which is used sixteen times in Proverbs. The combination of *towkechah* with the verb form *yakach* (reprove, Strongs, 3198, חָכַי), which occurs nine times, makes an obvious case for the large amount of verbal correction that should be used before the rod, which is only mentioned three times. No doubt, a delicate balance exists in the use of the rod and reproof. "Some give the rod without reproof, without any effort to produce sensibility of consciences" (Bridges, 1959, p. 571), which should be weighed when considering the New Testament command to refrain from provoking a child to anger (Ephesians 6:4). While the father may tend to be too hard on his child, generally mothers tend to be more sensitive (Sorenson, 2006, p. 273) which is why 29:15 speaks of a "child left to himself." The maternal sensitivity knows that her tender (4:3) child's body and character is sensitive because they are undeveloped and inexperienced (Waltke, 2004, p. 278). However, in order to avoid shame, a mother who is serious about teaching her child will instill wisdom by use of the rod when it is obvious that a child will not heed verbal reproof.

While the rod and reproof are negative means, rejoicing and respect are positive methods for teaching the child. In 23:25, the exhortation to "let your father and mother be glad; let her who bore you rejoice" uses the gladness of the father and the rejoicing of the mother as motivation for doing right. In 10:1 and 15:20 the text of Proverbs state that a "wise son makes a glad father, but a foolish son is a sorrow to his mother (but a foolish man despises his mother)." Proverbs 15:20 helpfully "describes the callousness of the one who inflicts grief on his mother" (Longman, 2008, p. 141). Not much should be made of the fact that the father is glad in these verses and the mother is sorrowing, because other Proverbs "ascribe grief to the father (17:21, 25) and joy to the mother (23:25)" (Waltke, 2004, p. 451). "The intended contrast, then, is not between joyful fathers and grieving mothers but between the honor or shame that comes to both parents based on their son's choices" (Koptak, 2003, p. 288). As the son understands the psychological impacts that his actions have on his parents, making them rejoice becomes a motivation for right doing (Waltke, 2004, p. 451). The rod gives an image of authority while rejoicing emphasizes the relational aspect between a mother and child. For this reason, the use of the rod may be best at a young age, while rejoicing and respect are effective for older children.

In the same text, 23:22 states, "Listen to your father who gave you life, and do not despise your mother when she is old." Although the specific word is not used, requiring "respect" is seen in verse 22 and greatly reinforced elsewhere in Proverbs. In bringing syntheses to all her methods, it is interesting to note that while these positive forms of reinforcement are useful, the rod is commended ten verses earlier (Miller, 2004, p. 232). The domestic instruction of 23:22-25 makes it clear that the mother deserves respect for two reasons: she "gave you life" and because "she is old." This encompasses the life of the parent's relationship to the son—from his birth to their old age. Their gray heads crown their lives in wisdom and for this they certainly deserve respect (Proverbs 16:31). While some have interpreted this proverb to focus on the son's responsibility to care for his elderly parents when they are physically incapable to do so themselves (Phillips, 1997, p. 232), it must be understood that the respect and honor asked of the heir is more transcending than just physical care during old age. The warning to respect one's mother is repeated throughout Proverbs. Destruction is promised for the one who would curse (20:20; 30:11), vandalize (19:26), rob (28:24), or mock (30:17) his mother. The above listed acts, which flow out of a lack of respect, should be of no surprise since "disrespect for parents, which leads to all sorts of ungodliness, is one of the signs of the distressing times to come (1 Tim. 3:1-4)" (Waltke, 2004, p. 259). "To shun parental discipline is to embark on a life characterized by lack of discipline and excessive violence, and such persons are naturally prone to die a violent death" (Garrett, 1993). The capstone verse that reinforces the respect due to mothers is in King Lemuel's accolade of 31:28 that says, "Her children rise up and call her blessed; her husband also, and he praises her."

It is entirely possible that the praise of the excellent wife by King Lemuel in 31:10-31 may be a reflection on his own mother (Jensen, 1976, p. 82).

Conclusion

This expositional examination has revealed *that* a mother plays a vital role in the teaching of her children and has further expounded on *what* she must do to steer the morals of her son and *how* she should go about doing so. This not only shows her importance in the home, but also highlights her impact on society and in the church. May Christian mothers realize their position within the ordained order of Creation and be challenged to take up this important task. "Woman, how divine your mission, here upon our natal sod; keep—oh, keep the young heart open always to the breath of God! ...For the hand that rocks the cradle is the hand that rocks the world."

References

Bridges, C. (1959). *An exposition of Proverbs* (pp. 571-617). Grand Rapids, MI: Zondervan.

Gammie, J., & Purdue, L. (1990). *The sage in Israel and the ancient near East* (p. 161). Winona Lake, IN: Eisenbrauns.

Gardner, M. (Ed.). (1995). *Famous poems from bygone days* (p. 153). New York, NY: Dover.

Garrett, D. (1993). *Proverbs, Ecclesiastes, Song of Songs: The new American commentary* (p. 240). Nashville, TN: Broadman & Holman.

Hubbard, D. (1991). *The communicator's commentary* (p. 49). Dallas, TX: W Pub Group.

Hughes, K. (2001). *Disciplines of a godly man.* Wheaton, IL: Crossway Books.

Jensen, I. (1976). *Proverbs: Bible self study guide* (p. 82). Chicago, IL: Moody Press.

Kidner, D. (1975). *The Proverbs: An introduction and commentary* (pp. 50-51). Downers Grove, IL: InterVarsity Press.

Kipling, R. (1995). *Plain tales from the hills* (p. 12). Garden City, SC: Doubleday Page and Company.

Koptak, P. (2003). *Proverbs: The NIV application commentary* (p. 288). Grand Rapids, MI: Zondervan.

Kroeger, C., & Evans, M. (Eds.). (2002). *The IVP women's Bible commentary* (p. 320). Downers Grove, IL: InterVarsity Press.

Longman III, T., & Garland, D. (Eds.). (2008). *The expositor's Bible commentary: Proverbs–Isaiah* (Revised ed., Vol. 6, pp. 47-141). Grand Rapids, MI: Zondervan.

Marion, L. (1996). *Modernization & the structure of societies* (Vol. 2). New Brunswick, NJ: Transaction.

Martin, J. (1995). *Proverbs: Old Testament guides* (p. 78-79). England: Sheffield Academic.

McKane, W. (1977). *Proverbs, a new approach* (p. 389). London: SCM Press LTD.

Miller, J. (2004). *Proverbs* (p. 232). Scottdale, PA: Herald Press.

Ortlund, R. (n.d.). Male-female equality and male headship Genesis 1-3. Retrieved May 1, 2015, from http://bible.org/seriespage/male-female-equality-and-male-headship-genesis-1-3.

Perowne, T. T. (1899). *The Proverbs: The Cambridge Bible for schools and colleges* (p. 186). London: Cambridge at the University Press.

Phillips, J. (1997). *Exploring Proverbs* (p. 232). Neptune, NJ: Kregel.

Sorenson, D. (2006). *The Proverbs: Godly advice for young adults* (p. 273). Duluth, MN: Northstar Ministries.

Waltke, B. (2004). *The Book of Proverbs: New International commentary on the Old Testament, Chapters 1-14* (pp. 278-451). Grand Rapids, MI: Wm. B. Eerdmans.

Waltke, B. (2004). *The Book of Proverbs: New International commentary on the Old Testament, Chapters 15-31* (p. 251). Grand Rapids, MI: Wm. B. Eerdmans.

Whybray, R. N. (1972). *The book of Proverbs: The Cambridge Bible commentary* (p. 181). Great Britain: Cambridge University Press.

Whybray, R. N. (1994). *The composition of the book of Proverbs* (p. 153). England: Sheffield Academic Press.

Author Biography

Daniel A. Webster is the Pastor of Glad Tidings Church in Asheboro, North Carolina.

The Excellent Wife
Table 2

5:15 Drink water from your own cistern, flowing water from your own well.

5:16 Should your springs be scattered abroad, streams of water in the streets?

5:18 Let your fountain be blessed, and rejoice in the wife of your youth,

5:19 a lovely deer, a graceful doe. Let her breasts fill you at all times with delight; be intoxicated always in her love.

11:16 A gracious woman gets honor, and violent men get riches.

12:4 An excellent wife is the crown of her husband, but she who brings shame is like rottenness in his bones.

14:1 The wisest of women builds her house, but folly with her own hands tears it down.

18:22 He who finds a wife finds a good thing and obtains favor from the LORD.

19:14 House and wealth are inherited from fathers, but a prudent wife is from the LORD.

30:19 the way of an eagle in the sky, the way of a serpent on a rock, the way of a ship on the high seas, and the way of a man with a virgin.

31:10 An excellent wife who can find? She is far more precious than jewels.

31:11 The heart of her husband trusts in her, and he will have no lack of gain.

31:12 She does him good, and not harm, all the days of her life.

31:13 She seeks wool and flax, and works with willing hands.

31:14 She is like the ships of the merchant; she brings her food from afar.

31:15 She rises while it is yet night and provides food for her household and portions for her maidens.

31:16 She considers a field and buys it; with the fruit of her hands she plants a vineyard.

31:17 She dresses herself with strength and makes her arms strong.

31:18 She perceives that her merchandise is profitable. Her lamp does not go out at night.

31:19 She puts her hands to the distaff, and her hands hold the spindle.

31:20 She opens her hand to the poor and reaches out her hands to the needy.

31:21 She is not afraid of snow for her household, for all her household are clothed in scarlet.

31:22 She makes bed coverings for herself; her clothing is fine linen and purple.

31:23 Her husband is known in the gates when he sits among the elders of the land.

31:24 She makes linen garments and sells them; she delivers sashes to the merchant.

31:25 Strength and dignity are her clothing, and she laughs at the time to come.

31:26 She opens her mouth with wisdom, and the teaching of kindness is on her tongue.

31:27 She looks well to the ways of her household and does not eat the bread of idleness.

31:29 "Many women have done excellently, but you surpass them all."

31:30 Charm is deceitful, and beauty is vain, but a woman who fears the LORD is to be praised.

31:31 Give her of the fruit of her hands, and let her works praise her in the gates.

The Quarrelsome Wife
Table 3

11:22 Like a gold ring in a pig's snout is a beautiful woman without discretion.

12:4 An excellent wife is the crown of her husband, but she who brings shame is like rottenness in his bones.

14:1 The wisest of women builds her house, but folly with her own hands tears it down.

19:13 A foolish son is ruin to his father, and a wife's quarreling is a continual dripping of rain.

21:9 It is better to live in a corner of the housetop than in a house shared with a quarrelsome wife.

21:19 It is better to live in a desert land than with a quarrelsome and fretful woman.

25:24 It is better to live in a corner of the housetop than in a house shared with a quarrelsome wife.

27:15 A continual dripping on a rainy day and a quarrelsome wife are alike;

27:16 to restrain her is to restrain the wind or to grasp oil in one's right hand.

30:21 Under three things the earth trembles; under four it cannot bear up:

30:22 a slave when he becomes king, and a fool when he is filled with food;

30:23 an unloved woman when she gets a husband, and a maidservant when she displaces her mistress.

The Adulterous Woman
Table 4

2:16 So you will be delivered from the forbidden woman, from the adulteress with her smooth words,

2:17 who forsakes the companion of her youth and forgets the covenant of her God;

2:18 for her house sinks down to death, and her paths to the departed;

2:19 none who go to her come back, nor do they regain the paths of life.

5:3 For the lips of a forbidden woman drip honey, and her speech is smoother than oil,

5:4 but in the end she is bitter as wormwood, sharp as a two-edged sword.

5:5 Her feet go down to death; her steps follow the path to Sheol;

5:6 she does not ponder the path of life; her ways wander, and she does not know it.

5:8 Keep your way far from her, and do not go near the door of her house,

5:20 Why should you be intoxicated, my son, with a forbidden woman and embrace the bosom of an adulteress?

6:24 to preserve you from the evil woman, from the smooth tongue of the adulteress.

6:25 Do not desire her beauty in your heart, and do not let her capture you with her eyelashes;

6:26 for the price of a prostitute is only a loaf of bread, but a married woman hunts down a precious life.

6:29 So is he who goes in to his neighbor's wife; none who touches her will go unpunished.

6:32 He who commits adultery lacks sense; he who does it destroys himself.

7:4 Say to wisdom, "You are my sister," and call insight your intimate friend,

7:5 to keep you from the forbidden woman, from the adulteress with her smooth words.

7:8 passing along the street near her corner, taking the road to her house

7:10 And behold, the woman meets him, dressed as a prostitute, wily of heart.

7:11 She is loud and wayward; her feet do not stay at home;

7:12 now in the street, now in the market, and at every corner she lies in wait.

7:13 She seizes him and kisses him, and with bold face she says to him,

7:14 "I had to offer sacrifices, and today I have paid my vows;

7:15 so now I have come out to meet you, to seek you eagerly, and I have found you.

7:16 I have spread my couch with coverings, colored linens from Egyptian linen;

7:17 I have perfumed my bed with myrrh, aloes, and cinnamon.

7:18 Come, let us take our fill of love till morning; let us delight ourselves with love.

7:19 For my husband is not at home; he has gone on a long journey;

7:20 he took a bag of money with him; at full moon he will come home."

7:21 With much seductive speech she persuades him; with her smooth talk she compels him.

7:22 All at once he follows her, as an ox goes to the slaughter, or as a stag is caught fast

7:25 Let not your heart turn aside to her ways; do not stray into her paths,

7:26 for many a victim has she laid low, and all her slain are a mighty throng

7:27 Her house is the way to Sheol, going down to the chambers of death.

22:14 The mouth of forbidden women is a deep pit; he with whom the LORD is angry will fall into it.

23:27 For a prostitute is a deep pit; an adulteress is a narrow well.

23:28 She lies in wait like a robber and increases the traitors among mankind.

29:3 He who loves wisdom makes his father glad, but a companion of prostitutes squanders his wealth.

30:20 This is the way of an adulteress: she eats and wipes her mouth and says, "I have done no wrong."

31:3 Do not give your strength to women, your ways to those who destroy kings.

Let No One Despise You For Your Elders: The Resolution of Youthful Rebellion and Elder Authority as Found in 1 Timothy

Christopher Talbot

Abstract: On a recent podcast, Carl Trueman, the Paul Woolley Professor of Church History at Westminster Theological Seminary, posited that 1 Timothy 4:12 may be the most incomprehensible verse in all of Scripture amidst our contemporary context. He states that within a culture that is so enamored with youth culture, it would be inconceivable for the church, let alone society-at-large, to despise those who actually are young. Broadly speaking, culture within the United States has an obsession with youth. Within this youth culture is the intrinsic need to rebel, especially against basic authorities. Phenomena such as extended adolescence and the juvenilization of American Christianity (Bergler, 2012) bring these problems immediately to the church's doorstep, if not inside. Yet, in our ministry to families, and youth in particular, we often herald 1 Timothy 4:12 as our ministerial mantra. We encourage youth to "let no one despise them," assuming a division and rebellion between youth and the rest of culture.

While we rightfully encourage youth to be prepared for possible coming derision, we must hold this exhortation in accordance to Paul's full teaching. That is to say, we must hold 1 Timothy 4:12 in tandem with the varied statements in 1 Timothy 5. It is the aim of this article to place 1 Timothy 4:12 in its correct context of Paul's admonition. In doing so, it will hold a biblical understanding of 1 Timothy 4:12 up and against a prevailing cultural interpretation of the text. Further, the article will explore how to keep our youth and family ministries from cultural syncretism by balancing ministries between an appreciation for youth and a respect for elder authority. This will conclude with the practical implications found therein.

Keywords: 1 Timothy, Authority, Elder, Ministry, Rebellion, Youth

Introduction

On a recent podcast, Dr. Carl Trueman, professor of Church History at Westminster Theological Seminary, satirically posited that 1 Timothy 4:12 may be the most incomprehensible passage in our modern American culture ("Forever Young"). That is, Trueman believes the first half of this particular verse falls flat on our contemporary ears: "Let no one despise you for your youth…" (English Standard Version, ESV). In opposition to the vast array of youth groups who herald this verse as their key mantra, he postulates that this verse is incomprehensible in a culture so obsessed with being and staying young. A cursory look at our culture easily demonstrates the infatuation with youthfulness. As one thinks about clothing selections, diet regimens, and pictures of the "good life" on our screens, one will quickly realize that youth is at the top of the American hierarchy of needs. Therefore, for one who desires youth to be despised by a society-at-large is as paradoxical as it is unexplainable.

However, one's concern should not stop there. Within current youth culture is an intrinsic foundation of rebellion, especially from basic roles of authority. At least since the sexual revolution of the 1960s and the paradigm shift toward embracing postmodernism in the United States, subsequent generations have rejected not only epistemological authority, but also parental. While these various rejections of authority may seem arbitrary at first, it is plausible to believe the philosophical and practical are deeply related. Thus, for our cultural milieu to desire youth is to reject elder generations and their fundamental authority. Immediately one can observe the implications for youth and family ministry. To reject the spiritual authority of previous generations is to reject the model we have for family discipleship (cf. Dueteronomy 6; Ephesians 6).

For these reasons it is the focus of this article to explore the themes of youthful rebellion and elder authority as found in 1 Timothy, while concurrently drawing implications from and for contemporary culture. It is also within aim of this article to posit a resolution of Paul's themes as found in his epistle to young Timothy, his adopted-son in the faith. By doing so, our aim should be to manifest a counter-cultural spiritual authority that seeks to transform subsequent generations rather than conform them to society.

Youthful Rebellion

As we dissect our understanding of youthful rebellion and its cultural implications, it cannot be understated how much philosophical ideals have influenced and affected the home—specifically the parental structure. That is to say, one must take a close look at how the external philosophies of a given culture have made impact on the internal values of the home. If the culture-at-large is moving toward societal degradation, the family will follow suit unless they articulate a counter-cultural alternative. Furthermore, if external culture is rejecting any and all non-subjective epistemological authority, it would be plausible that the rejection of parental authority would walk in tandem—an authority that exists outside the particular person.

Biblical Background

An important element in understanding the authorial rebellion of youth is to paint a correct exegetical understanding of 1 Timothy 4:12. A biblical understanding of this specific verse is vital in understanding its common use in our current context. As any, this verse is translated in a variety of ways. To begin, there is some diversity in opinion as to what "youth" denotes. While there are a few theories, the term "youth" most likely implies that Timothy was younger than Paul, or younger than the elders of the church (Towner, 2006, p. 314). In any case, it is clear from the plain reading of the text that Timothy's relative age caused a burden in a culture that promoted some type of age veneration (Towner, 2006, p. 314). What is important to note here, however, is that the age veneration of Timothy's context is the exact reversal of our modern society, but the tension is timeless. John Stott writes concerning this verse, "Older people have always found it difficult to accept young people as responsible adults in their own right, let alone as leaders. And young people are understandably irritated when their elders keep reminding them of their immaturity and inexperience, and treat them with contempt" (Stott, 1996, p.119).

Yet, it is worth commenting that Paul's admonition in light of Timothy's youth is not to regress deeper into his adolescence, but rather set an example for believers—that is, he is to strive for exemplary spiritual maturity. While he may be despised for his youth, Paul is encouraging Timothy to not let age define his ministry. Simply put, to focus on Timothy's youth in the verse is to miss, and even polarize, the truth. The focus of this verse is to exhort young Timothy to spiritual adulthood particularly in the way that he sets a pattern for his congregants to follow. It is a call, first and foremost, to godly character (Hughes, 2000, p. 115). As H. A. Ironside emboldens readers, "Do not develop an inferiority complex because you are younger than some of those to whom you minister... A young man may be very immature in some respects, but if he is characterized by these things [1 Tim. 4:12]... he will not have to try to compel others to accord him recognition" (Ironside, 1947, p. 107). Thus, as we look at 1 Timothy 4:12 for encouragement in youth and family ministry, it should not serve to encourage extended adolescence or immaturity. Rather, it exhorts us to maturity, even in light of relative youthfulness.

Philosophy and Parenting

By laying an exegetical foundation from this verse, one can now seek to comprehend how our understanding has been changed concerning youth and authority. Tedd Tripp, author of *Shepherding a Child's Heart,* has insightful comments concerning the themes of youth and authority. He writes, "Today's parents are part of the generation that threw off authority. The racial and anti-war protests of the 1960s powerfully shaped their ideas. The protest movement took on the establishment. It changed the way we think about authority and the rights of the individual" (1995, p. xvii). What Tripp is stating is simple, yet profound. While one can muse that parenting and philosophy may have connections, Tripp is drawing a straight line between the two. He argues that those who rejected modernism and embraced postmodernism during the sexual revolution of the 1960s are the same ones who are raising kids today. Therefore, what was once a philosophical idea is now being fleshed out in parental authority— or the lack thereof. As Tripp notes, this redraws our ideas about authority in the life of the person.

While Tripp is making a critique, he is concurrently opening a door to a solution. The parent is the one who was impacted by the postmodern philosophical ideas of generations past, but the parent also has the ability to recalibrate those ideas. As Kenda Creasy Dean says, our current "cultural conditions of postmodernity require the church to function as a bilingual community, conversant in both the traditions of the church and the narratives of the dominant culture" (2010, p. 112). It is obvious that parents are perfectly and providentially poised to be those "translators." Dean argues for parents to work as the cultural interpreters for their children. Parents alone possess the authority in their child's life to lead them into understanding society *via* a biblical worldview—away from the damaging philosophies that may have ensnared them generations ago.

We should note that teens, in some way, instinctively "master the culture" around them. They are able to understand profound levels of the culture in stages of detail and nuance (Dean, p. 122). They quickly, and almost intuitively, take ownership of the way their current culture operates and moves. Yet, they have never lived outside of their current culture and often fail to have the faculties to immediately understand an alternative path. For that reason, parents are best poised to span the gap for their children, holding the authoritative understanding of culture from their own experience, and also the authoritative position in church and home, and thus are able to "translate" their understanding for their children.

Media as Mother

Before moving on to a full resolution of the rebellion of youth culture, it is important to note how youth are most often impacted in their cultural environment. It is no overstatement to argue that media, in its various forms, holds the highest sway over the majority of American youth. Walt Mueller writes, "Media provides the emerging generations with 'maps of reality' to guide them into adulthood" (2006, p. 27). Never before have youth gained more of their basic understanding of the world from media than today. The impact is often exhaustive. From political values to social justice issues, media can have a powerful effect on how youth understand and interpret the world around them. Not least of these is how media often portrays the traditional family and the structure therein. As Chap Clark points out, sitcoms like *Modern Family* portray three "alternative" family structures. As he explains, "Over time the idea of family—what it is, who (or what) is included, and why it matters—has slowly relegated to private opinion, creating a sociological and cultural divide (2011, p. 92).

Yet, the church is not helpless at the hands of modern media. Marva Dawn boldly states, "In the Christian community we want to be decisively different, for we know that formation of alternative character takes a great investment of time to counteract all the influence of the dominant culture" (1997, p.120). She writes elsewhere, "Do parents realize that one of their primary callings in life is to invest time in the training of their children?... I constantly wonder why so many parents keep serving their children garbage for their spiritual dinner" (Dawn, 1997, p. 175). Unfortunately, one can easily fail in this regard. According to Mark DeVries, "Only *15 percent* of men between the ages of forty and fifty-nine have a mature, integrated faith" (emphasis added, 2005, p. 73). As is the case too often, the critiques are easy to observe, but the solution is considerably more difficult. For this reason, one must turn their attention toward a more mature faith and its consequent authority.

Elder Authority

Rather than swing the pendulum and merely find a reactionary point, it is important to look for a balanced resolution to the stated problem. If, as the thesis states, youthful rebellion is on the rise, to what biblical solution can one arrive? Furthermore, one must analyze what paradigm shifts may be required within their current parental framework. Lastly, it is necessary to calibrate authority within its biblical definition rather than a cultural contortion.

Biblical Foundations

Thankfully, Scripture has again not left one to their own devices when seeking a biblical solution. While 1 Timothy 4:12 mentions youth, Paul continues the theme of age and maturity elsewhere. Much of this is found in the fifth chapter of Paul's letter to Timothy. For example, 1 Timothy 5:1-2, "Do not rebuke an older man but encourage him as you would a father, younger men as brothers, older women as mothers, younger women as sisters, in all purity" (ESV). Likewise, 1 Timothy 5:17, "Let the elders who rule well be considered worthy of double honor, especially those who labor in preaching and teaching" (ESV). It would seem Paul is striving for a balanced perspective between youthful ambition and elderly wisdom.

Most scholars agree that in Timothy's context "elders" were highly regarded—something hard for our culture to grasp (Fee, 1988, p. 107). So much so, Paul's admonition to Timothy in 4:12 may have been in part to counterbalance the veneration of those who were older. To demonstrate, while Timothy is called "young" in this verse, Timothy was probably in his thirties—an adult by today's standards. We, however, like to reserve the word "young" for those in their teens and early twenties (Liefield, 1999, p.165). This simple clarification exhibits the reversal of the culture of their time to our own. Moreover, the emphasis on elder authority is not limited to this singular epistle. Paul's admonition for parental authority is a theme throughout Scripture (Deuteronomy 4:10, 11:19; Proverbs 19:18; Matthew 15:4; Colossians 3:20; Ephesians 6:1-3).

Tedd Tripp writes, "As a parent, you have authority because God calls you to be an authority in your child's life. You have the authority to act on behalf of God" (1995, p. 29). The nuance on authority in Tripp's statement is vital. It is not a tyrannical leadership a parent exercises, but rather a leadership based on the stewardship of God's authority. He writes elsewhere, "The parenting task is multi-faceted. It involves being authorities who are kind, shepherding your children to understand themselves in God's world, and keeping the gospel in clear view so your children can internalize the good news and someday live in mutuality with you as people under God" (1995, p. xvii).

One quickly realizes that the authority parents have over their children manifests itself as something distinctly countercultural—away from present understandings of "authority." This authority, as Tripp mentions, is wonderfully multi-faceted. It is more than a simple pragmatic model to transmit virtues. The authority a parent stewards is, in many ways, a demonstration of the virtues of God. In the book *Children Matter*, the authors write, "Wise, loving, consistent discipline lays the foundation for children to understand God's laws, judgment, mercy and grace" (May, Posterski, Stonehouse, & Cannell, 2005, p. 158). This being said, it comes at no surprise to realize that parents exercise the single most important role in the development of their children (DeVries, 2004, p. 62).

Parental Paradigms

In order to practice biblical, parental authority, it is important to note the paradigm shift that is required for parents and churches in this process. Contrary to common belief, Christian parents are poised and ready to be the primary disciplers of their children (see figure 1).

Figure 1

FAMILY DISCIPLESHIP PERCEPTIONS AND PRACTICES SURVEY PARENTAL PERCEPTIONS OF SPIRITUAL RESPONSIBILITY (Jones, 2011, p. 99)						
	Strongly Disagree	Disagree	Somewhat Disagree	Somewhat Agree	Agree	Strongly Agree
The church is where ought to receive most of their Bible Teaching	26 percent	45 percent	17 percent	10 percent	2 percent	1 percent
When my child sponanteously asks a biblical or theological question, I really wish that my child would have asked a minister or other church leader instead of me	61 percent	31 percent	3 percent	2 percent	2 percent	2 percent
Parents, and particularly fathers, have a responsibility to engage personally in a discipleship process with each of their children	0 percent	0 percent	0 percent	4 percent	34 percent	62 percent
Minister or other church leaders are the people primarily responsible for discipline of my children and teaching them to share the Gospel with others	37 percent	44 percent	11 percent	6 percent	0 percent	1 percent

According to Jones' study displayed in figure 1, it would seem that a sizable majority of parents acknowledge their God-given role in the life of their children. So, then, what changes must parents make in the way they exhibit authority to their children? Change occurs in bridging the gap between different types of parental authority. Alex Chediak writes,

> Positional authority is God-given; moral authority must be earned over time. Think of moral authority as the permission to speak into the inner core of someone's heart—to shape the person's heart and, in turn life. We must win the hearts of our teens so that they *want* us involved in their lives, leading them into adulthood, interpreting the fast-paced biological and social changes they're experiencing, helping them process their shortcomings and insecurities, and encouraging them that with God's help they can do great things (Chediak, 2014, p. 6).

Authority, then, requires action and commitment on the part of the parent. There is a different type of "translation" that must happen between parent and child. The parent is not only present to help formulate the child's Christian worldview. They also translate by building a personal, moral bridge between them and the child. Chap Clark notes that the majority of conflicts between parent and child seem to be about the dynamics of their relationship, rather than a specific issue (2011, p. 99). Exercising the proper relationship, as all actions of faith, can be daunting. "Whenever we participate in the transmission of faith, across cultures or *generations*, we are putting the gospel into the hands of people new to it" [emphasis added] (Dean, p. 128).

One must come to realize that the parent-child relationship is foundational for nearly all of life. The parent-child bond is worldview forming and divinely-ordained. Childhood and parenthood are dependent upon one another for their very definition. "There is a tendency to define childhood apart from serious reflection on the meaning of parenthood. Yet a moment's pause might lead one to recognize that there is hardly a deeper characteristic of human life than the parent-child relationship... The Christian faith would have us look more closely at the fundamental parent-child nexus. Yet in the churches far too little discussion is given over the vocation of parenthood and the child's obligations to parents" (Guroian, 2001, pp. 61-62). Again, Paul's instruction to Timothy solidifies this point. Timothy's youthfulness and the elders' authority were both contingent on each other. Therefore, Paul's admonition for youth to seek maturity and elders to lead are inseparable. These responsibilities rely on each other to be fulfilled by either party. Youth must strive for maturity, but elders, or parents in this case, must practice authority.

Helping, Not Hurting

The parent-child relationship is foundational to this argument, but is ultimately futile if we do not have a biblically robust definition of authority (Tripp, 1995, p. 29). The word authority, as we understand it in Scripture, is primarily a New Testament term. It is predominantly the word *exousia* and is used in one of four ways. The *Baker Theological Dictionary of the Bible* defines authority in one way as, "the sphere in which authority is exercised." The writer continues,

> The question of authority is a fundamental issue facing every person, especially the believer. Its significance cannot be overestimated. Every person has an authority in life that he or she submits to as a subordinate, not by constraint but by conviction... How, then, does God exercise his authority over creation and his creatures? The testimony of Scripture is that God has established three fundamental spheres of authority within which he delegates authority to individuals. These spheres are civil government, *the home*, and the church. The believer is obliged to obey those holding authority in those realms. Citizens are to submit to the governing authorities (1 Peter 2:13-14). Children are to obey parents (Eph. 6:1-2) [emphasis added] (Hamstra, 1996, pp. 45-46).

Authority, then, is essential to the entire Christian faith. To follow or steward authority in the home is but an extension of the tenant God has ordained in one's life. Tedd Tripp articulates it well when he writes, "The purpose of your authority in the lives of your children is not to hold them under your power; but to empower them to be self-controlled people living freely under the authority of God" (Tripp, 1995, p. xviii). Thus, we come full circle. To exercise proper parental (elder) authority is to exhibit the accurate values of God. And to exhibit these values, is to provide an example for youth striving to be spiritually mature.

Conclusion

It has been the aim of this article to bring balance to an otherwise difficult topic. While culture-at-large may or may not continue to be infatuated with the fountain of youth, Scripture has given another option. In place of rebellious adolescence, Scripture has exhorted all, no matter the age, to a life of spiritual maturity. Thus, if one is young, they are called to push against the culture and seek a more mature life of spiritual character. If one is older, specifically parents, they are charged with a particular role of overseeing and guiding their children. As Tedd Tripp writes, "Teach your children that God loves them so much that he gave them parents to be kind authorities to teach and lead them" (Tripp, 1995, p. 33). We do this by tying all of our authority and exercise thereof distinctly to the commands and statutes of Scripture (Tripp, 1995, p. 39).

In other words, let us tell one another, "let no one despise you for your elders," for they have been placed in the lives of believers to exercise oversight and instruction. It is by the stewardship of God that they are able to instruct those that are younger than them. Instead of jettisoning the past, may believers—young and old alike—seek to find instruction and help in the generations before them.

References

Chediak, A. (2014). *Preparing your teens for college: Faith, friends, finances, and much more.* Carol Stream, IL: Tyndale House.

Clark, C. (2011). *Hurt 2.0: Inside the world of today's teenagers.* Grand Rapids, MI: Baker Academic.

Dawn, M. J. (1997). *Is it a lost cause? Having the heart of God for the church's children.* Grand Rapids, MI: Eerdmans.

Dean, K. C. (2010). *Almost Christian: What the faith of our teenagers is telling the American church.* New York, NY: Oxford University Press.

DeVries, M. (2004). *Family-based youth ministry, revised and expanded.* Downers Grove, IL: InterVaristy Press.

Fee, G. (1988). *1 and 2 Timothy, Titus.* Peabody, MA: Hendrickson.

Guroian, V. "The ecclesial family: John Chrysostom on parenthood and children" ed. Marcia J. Bunge. in (2001). *The Child in Christian Thought.* Grand Rapids, MI: Eerdmans.

Hamstra, S. Jr. (1996). "Authority" in Elwell, W. A. (ed.) *Baker Theological Dictionary of the Bible.* Grand Rapids, MI: Baker Books.

Hughes, K., & Chappell, B. (2000). *1 & 2 Timothy and Titus: To guard the deposit.* Wheaton, IL: Crossway Books.

Ironside, H.A. (1947). *Timothy, Titus, and Philemon.* Neptune, NJ; Loizeaux Brothers, Inc.

Jones, T. P. (2011). *Family ministry field guide: How your church can equip parents to make disciples.* Indianapolis, IN: Wesleyan.

Kostenberger, A., & Wilder, T. (2010). *Entrusted with the Gospel: Paul's theology in the pastoral epistles.* Nashville, TN: B&H Academic.

Liefield, W. L. (1999). *The NIV application commentary: 1 and 2 Timothy, Titus.* Grand Rapids, MI: Zondervan.

May, S., Posterski, B., Stonehouse, C., & Cannell, L. (2005). *Children matter: Celebrating their place in the church, family, and community.* Grand Rapids, MI: Eerdmans.

Mueller, W. (2006). *Engaging the soul of youth culture: Bridging teen worldviews and Christian truth.* Downers Grove, IL: IVP Books.

Stott, J. (1996). *Guard the truth: The message of 1 Timothy & Titus.* Downers Grove, IL: InterVarsity Press.

Towner, P. H. (2006). *The letters to Timothy and Titus.* Grand Rapids, MI: Eerdmans.

Tripp, T. (1995). *Shepherding a child's heart.* Wapwallopen, PA: Shepherd Press.

Trueman, C., Pruitt, T., & Byrd, A. (2015, May 27). Forever young. *Mortification of Spin.* Podcast retrieved from: http://www.alliancenet.org/mos/podcast/37070.

Author Biography

Chris Talbot is the Program Coordinator for Youth and Family Ministry at Welch College in Nashville, Tennessee.

Practitioner Insights

The D6 Family Journal editorial board helped design the uniqueness of this journal. This section entitled Practitioner Insights offers you a look at family ministry from practitioners engaged in preschool, children, student, college, adults, or senior ministry. The practitioner reflections do not submit to the same academic peer review process but still pass through multiple editors before becoming part of the volume. We believe this section will allow insightful ministry leaders the chance to present an area facing the church today.

The New Traditional Family
Leneita Fix

Tears welled up as she hid her face. What had been a jovial conversation while sitting on the beach suddenly turned serious. We discussed the challenges of raising adolescents in this day and age and I watched the fear cross her brow. "I just don't know if we are making the right decisions for our son, I don't want him to grow up a failure." The deep concern of this Mom surprised me, however. She and her husband have a deep relationship with Christ, are affluent, and have been married for nearly 17 years. They carry all of the skills and qualities those of us in family ministry believe will raise anything but a failure.

I live in the tension myself, both of parenting four kids between the ages of 13-22 and working with parents and families. As my own children have grown older, I have grappled with that same pain of wondering if my children can be successful both in their relationship with the Lord and in life in general. Coming to grips with my own worries has caused me to realize how much I have judged other parents. You see I work in an area where the divorce rate is high and the number of cohabiting non-married parents is higher.[1] The two parent household with all children belonging to the couple that lives there has become a distant memory.[2] I have pointed my fingers and said, "If you could just be like us then your issues in parenting would be fixed."

Since the time of my high horse statements I have come to see we are all more alike than I ever knew. Parents as a rule love their children desperately and want the best for them. Sometimes two parent households where both have a vibrant relationship with Christ still end up with a child who is an addict due to nothing they have done wrong. Approximately 2.7 million grandparents in America today are the primary care-givers of their grandchildren, and I doubt any of them would say that was their first choice of their family situation.[3] Whether it is the Mom sitting with me on the beach or a single Mom, we all want our children to be happy and healthy. Yet, I am beginning to realize the idea of family is no longer simple.

No matter how we feel about what the perfect family should look like, the reality is that the non-traditional family is sitting in our pews and buying homes behind the church property. Due to the changing world around us, we no longer can identify the definitive "other side of the tracks" with a particular set of problems. Parents long for their children to grow up and be a successful member of society, whoever they are.

This is not to say God's plan has not always been for the family to be whole. Adam and Eve were made for each other literally and the plan was for them to "be fruitful and multiply." They never got the chance to bring children into Eden. Instead, the first family brought sin into the world, broke our relationship with the Lord, and their son was a murderer. Since that moment the Lord has been on the path of redeeming us, both individually and as a family. I do believe, however, we must come to terms with the reality that the family unit may take on another shape due to necessity. It is not always due to poor personal choices or personal sin that people find themselves in a different type of family.

Let us take the example of stay-at-home mothers. When I got pregnant with my first baby I was told in my own church if I wanted the best for my children I would quit working outside of my household and stay at home. According to the United States Department of Treasury, we entered a severe financial crisis between 2007-2009 that caused almost 8.8 million jobs to be lost and almost 19.1 trillion dollars of household income to be lost as well. The reality became that mothers entered the job force out of necessity. My husband and I have been called to ministry together since before we ever thought of starting a family. Our belief was that upon giving birth I would stay home with the babies. Originally, I came back to paid ministry feeling it was what God had called me to do. Then one day a friend of mine told me, "If you really love your children you will quit your ministry job and just be with them." My husband and I decided to pray and see if this was what Jesus was saying to us. On a practical level, when we looked at our budget we could not afford for me to quit. Even if I stopped working in ministry I would need to find a way to bring a paycheck home. This was not because I was driven to have a career or because we lived outside of our means. This was the tight rope between a rising cost of living and low paying roles. The economy has changed the labor force of the family out of necessity. It should not shock us then that almost 70 percent of all women in 2013 with children under the age of 18 were in the labor force.[4] More than 40 percent of mothers in 2014 were the primary breadwinners for their households.[5] By far, the most common arrangement today is for married parents in dual-income families with children under 18 to work. Around 67.8 percent of married mothers and 93.7 percent of married fathers served in the labor force.[6] Our family was blessed that since both my husband and I were working together, our children never had to enter daycare. However, I have friends who have had to put their children into daycare, while everyday it breaks their heart that someone else gets to witness the firsts of their "baby." Our society of dual working parents does not mean that they do not care about their children and do not want what is best for them. It is no longer a choice of whether or not a Mom would like to stay home. To meet the basic needs of the household, two salaries are often required.

If there is one thing the statistics of dual working parents prove, it is that most families carry burdens we will never see. Still, as practitioners, we can continue making judgments on decisions parents make for their family. We see them for a moment in passing at pick up and drop off for children's church and youth group and decide it is obvious by the life they live their hearts are not to disciple their children. Yet, I am finding more and more parents, who like myself and my friend, merely feel inadequate. They compare themselves to what they are told makes a "solid Christian" family and they are falling short. Instead of offering a hand up, we simply reaffirm their belief they are not good enough for their kids. Then those of us in ministry are frustrated when it feels like they are "passing the parenting" to those of us who hold a position that reaches into the lives of their children.

It is time that we make a choice to walk with every family no matter who they are. Our job as the body of Christ is to help each family know this begins with a relationship with Jesus. When the parents understand what it means to belong to the Lord, the family unit changes radically. I have come to realize, I must come to terms that families do not look like they once did and yet we have a common connection. None of us want to raise failures. The question we must ask is if we trust that God is big enough to continue to bring the broken and hurting back into relationship with Himself? Will we have faith the Lord loves each person in each family more than we ever possibly could? If we do, then could we do whatever it will take to walk with families in practical life giving ways?

Endnotes

[1]"Florida among U.S. States with the Highest Divorce Rates." WPBF. N.p., 20 Aug. 2013. Web. 02 July 2015.

[2]"Cohabitation Less Taboo, More Common among Dating Couples Who Become Pregnant—JusticeNewsFlash.com." JusticeNewsFlash.com. N.p., 07 Jan. 2014. Web. 02 July 2015.

[3]US Census Bureau.

[4]"Employment Characteristics of Families—2013," US Bureau of Labor Statistics press release, April 25, 2014.

[5]The Council of Economic Advisors. "Nine Facts About American Families and Work" (June 2014).

[6]US Census Bureau. "Table FG1: Married Couple Family Groups, By Labor Force Status of Both Spouses, and Race and Hispanic Origin of the Reference Person: 2014," America's Families and Living Arrangements: 2014: Family Groups (2014).

Author Biography

Leneita Fix is the missions/training coordinator for BowDown Church and Urban Youth Impact in West Palm Beach, Florida. She is the author of *The Beautiful Chaos of Parenting Teens: Navigating the Hardest Years You Will Ever Love*, *No Teenager Left Behind*, and *Everybody's Urban*. She has spoken to national audiences at conferences and churches such as D6, Simply Youth Ministry, Indiana State United Methodist Conference, Christian Community Development Association, as well as several local and national trainings.

Pastoral Perspective
Help, Pastor, My Son Is Gay!
Adam Clagg

How do we respond when a parent reaches out to us because her teenage son is gay? We, in family ministry, help navigate families through all sorts of issues… and sexuality is a major one. In the past, many Christian families did not discuss sex very often and they certainly did not involve their ministers. As Jonathan Parnell (2015) points out, homosexuality is not like other sins. It is different from other sins *right now* because it is celebrated by our larger society everywhere we look.

Let us examine the case study mentioned in the first sentence. From a pastor's perspective, I would recommend meeting with the family right away. The purpose of this meeting is to bring the love and power of the gospel into the highly emotional situation. At this point, we know very little, just what we received from the mother's text messages and phone calls. I like to meet at the church because most of their conversations about this been at the home. Plus, a café or coffee shop is too public to talk about this issue. The church is a neutral ground where people tend to behave themselves.

The teenager will more than likely believe you are on his mother's side. You already have a few strikes against you since you are an adult, an authority figure, and a minister. It is important to remember that you have no idea what either one has said to the other. You also do not know what they understand about biblical teaching of sexuality, sin, confession, and forgiveness. Most teens do not want to talk about sex in front of their parents and most people will not tell the whole truth when it involves their own sin. Remember the wise words of television character Dr. Gregory House, on House M.D., "Everybody lies."

Here is what I would do:

1. Reassure him that he is loved by God, his family, and his church. It does not matter what has been said or done in the past, nothing will

change this love. I would explain the importance of God's love, family love, and congregational love.

2. Explain my role as a pastoral counselor. I am not a licensed therapist. I am the family's minister and I am here to help. My job is to help mother and son communicate. When emotions are high, we do not hear things correctly or say what we mean to say. I am in the room to help them by watching facial expressions and body language to see if communication is sent and received correctly. If something has not been said or understood in a clear manner, it is my job to interrupt and make sure they both understand what was just said. I will ask them to tell you what happened and try their best not to interrupt each other. I need to listen carefully as they explain what happened to cause the mother to text you (Was he caught looking at pornography? Did He come out? Is she misunderstanding something he said or did?). I will ask for permission to take notes, and then summarize it to them to make sure you completely understand.

3. Share God's Word. Only 45 percent of those who regularly attend church read the Bible more than once a week. I would assume that neither one has a complete understanding of the Bible's teaching on lust and homosexuality. Depending on their specific situation, I would choose some Scriptures that apply to the situation. Having a printout of the Bible passages to give to the family is good. I may read some of these aloud or have each of us read some aloud.

Lust: Romans 7:14-25; 1 John 2:16; Galatians 5:19-21

Homosexuality: Genesis 19:1-13; Leviticus 18:22, 20:13; Judges 19:22; Romans 1:26-27; 1 Corinthians 6:9

4. Explain your church's theology of homosexuality. As a minister, it is your job to understand and be able to communicate your church's doctrine. With this and other doctrines, you may want to write down and practice talking about what you believe. Based on my church doctrine, I would probably say something like this:

God is love. He really does care about you and so do we. We care about you so much that we want to help you understand what God has taught us about this. We love you enough to tell you the truth and show you when you are wrong. We are a Bible-believing church. Homosexuality is a topic discussed in the Bible. It is never said to be a good thing, always bad, always a sin. Our understanding of life comes from God's Word. We cannot make up our own truth. Jesus said that God's Word is truth (John 17:17). God created everything and He makes the rules. Regarding homosexuality, here is what we believe, based on the Bible's teachings.

Human beings are created with the desire and ability to have sex. God designed sex for married people to enjoy and to create babies (Genesis 2:18, 25; 1 Corinthians 7:2-5). Because Adam and Eve sinned in the Garden of Eden, we are all born with a sin force inside of us. Each person (saved and unsaved) has temptations to sin. Some people have strong temptations to lie, others have strong temptations to steal, while others have strong temptations to lust. This is why you may feel you were born this way. Yes, everyone was born a sinner, but we do not have to give in to our temptations (1 Corinthians 10:13). Just because you may have temptations regarding same sex attraction or have even sinned, it does not mean you are gay. It means you are dealing with a temptation to sin just like everyone does (Hebrews 4:15-16).

Regarding the sin of homosexuality, there are different levels of involvement. First is an attraction to a person of the same sex. There are many documented reasons why you may feel an attraction to a specific boy or man. This is a topic for future discussion. Next is a temptation of same sex attraction. This is when you are attracted to more than just one man. You like guys. You may also like girls, but you have a sexual attraction to guys. Neither one of these things are sin. They are temptations. Giving in to temptation is sin. All sin separates us from God and causes problems in our lives (James 1:14-15). The next level is lust. This is when you fantasize about guys sexually. Another level is closely related. It is masturbation. Most fantasies will quickly escalate into masturbation, many times using pornography as a tool. Sexual fantasies about someone you are not married to is considered sin because Jesus said if we commit sexual sins in our heart it is the same as doing it in real life (Matthew 5:27-28). Another level is sexual contact with another guy. Touching, petting, kissing, making out, etc. is considered the sin of immorality. Any type of sex (oral, anal, or intercourse) is the sin of fornication (1 Corinthians 6:9-10).

That is what God has taught us about sexual sin. He has also taught us that He can forgive any sin. He also teaches us that we can escape any temptations to sin by running from the situation (1 Corinthians 10:13). I know the struggle you are experiencing has been very difficult. I know it is difficult now. And I know it will continue to be difficult. Through the power of Jesus, you can overcome this sin and have victory. The way you overcome this sin is the same way any of us overcome any sin… we confess it and repent. We confess to each other and we confess it to God. Then we repent, which means to turn away. We have to say no to the sin and say yes to God. Same sex attraction cannot just be prayed away. It will take time and will be a constant temptation, but Jesus can give you the victory!

Now, I know what I have just said is very different than what you may have heard from television, movies, school, society, friends, and discussion forums. What I have just shared with you is the truth from the God who made you and the God who loves you. Just because you have these temptations does not mean you are gay. Just because you may have acted on these temptations and sinned, does not mean you are gay. The world wants to define you by your thoughts and actions. God is the only one who can really define you and give you meaning, because He is the creator. He defines you as His son. Someone who has a purpose in life and can be successful, happy, and godly.

After explaining what the Bible teaches about sexual sin, I will ask if he has any questions. In all likelihood, he has not told me everything. Based on the entire situation, I will either set a date to meet again or talk about referring him to a Christian counselor. Here are some good resources to help this family:

Ministering in a Changing Sexual Landscape by Eddie Moody, Randall House (2015)

Focus on the Family Counselor Locator http://www.focusonthefamily.com/counseling/find-a-counselor.aspx

References

Parnell, J. (2014, April 21). "Why homosexuality is not like other sins." *Desiring God*. Retrieved October 5, 2015 from http://www.desiringgod.org/articles/why-homosexuality-is-not-like-other-sins.

House, M.D. Fox Entertainment. 2004-2012.

Stetzer, E. (2015, July 6). "The epidemic of Bible illiteracy in our churches." *The Exchange*. Retrieved November 1, 2015 from http://www.christianitytoday.com/edstetzer/2015/july/epidemic-of-bible-illiteracy-in-our-churches.html.

Author Biography

Dr. Adam Clagg pastors Covenant Church, near Chattanooga, Tennessee. He was one of the first students to receive the Master of Arts in Youth and Family Ministry from Lee University in 2004. He enjoys serving his local community on several boards and committees. Adam can be reached through his blog EveryLeader.Org or on Twitter Adam_Clagg.

Book Reviews

The book reviews submitted offer a critique of some of the latest family ministry titles. If you would like to see a title reviewed in the future, please submit at least two copies of either the book or galley copy (Publisher's PDF proof is acceptable if not yet published or to galley stage).

The DNA of D6: Building Blocks of Generational Discipleship. By Ron Hunter
Jr. Nashville, Tennessee: Randall House. 2015. 144 pp. $14.99. paper.

Review by Daniel Edwards, Lead Pastor at Faith Church in Chandler, Indiana. Daniel also serves as the Promotional Director for the Indiana State
Association of Free Will Baptists.

Anyone who has heard Ron Hunter speak of Generational Discipleship has likely picked up on his passion for this subject. Anyone who reads *The DNA of D6* will as well. It is clear from the beginning of the book that this is very personal work. Matt Markins' preface confirms the investment that Ron Hunter has made in the generational discipleship and family ministry movements. However, this is no manifesto. As personal as *The DNA of D6* is to Hunter, the better adjective to describe this work is practical. The material is communicated for the purpose of application and the content, strategies, and even the analogies serve that purpose. *The DNA of D6* achieves a high level of practicality by addressing churches of all shapes, establishing a biblical basis, driving home the end goal, building concrete action steps, and encouraging leaders past the challenges and hurdles they face. These components build a strong guide for leaders looking to shift their organization's strategy toward discipling the next generation within the family.

Chapters entitled "Staffing for A D6 Church" and "The Unseen Staff Member" might give the impression that Hunter has written to a narrow demographic of churches, but churches of every size will appreciate Hunter's approach in addressing all churches. The chapter on staffing makes it clear that the staff may be paid hires or a volunteer team, but the principles and strategy are the same. The unseen staff member is *Spoiler Alert* actually curriculum. The idea is curriculum can serve as an unseen (and relatively unpaid) staff member. Not only does this book prove to be practical to churches of all budget and team sizes, it also speaks to churches at any point on the generational discipleship spectrum. A church leader need not be an early adopter of the family ministry model or even use D6's curriculum to gain insights from Hunter on leading their church to follow the call of discipleship within family units. A commitment to help churches and leaders start where they are and head in the right direction is further demonstrated in the free use of a *DNA of D6 Generational Discipleship Assessment* tool that the book points to in the first chapter. Any church and every leader can find their place on the spectrum and follow the insights in the book to lead their church, big or small/multi-staff to bi-vocational pastor, in the direction of families discipling their own children.

With helps to establish where each reader might find themselves or their church and an obvious direction introduced early in the text, the author then establishes a biblical basis for the generational discipleship model. Since D6 stands for Deuteronomy 6, the reader will not be surprised that this passage is the launching point. Yet, Hunter establishes that Deuteronomy 6 is not merely a proof text. Deuteronomy 6 serves as the thesis for the strategy, but the movement is not short on passages for inspiration and instruction. Covering Genesis to Revelation positive and negative examples are sighted, commands and exhortations to parents are pointed out, and principles of influence stewardship are underscored. The chapter heading "D6 Goes Beyond Deuteronomy 6" is fitting. Readers will gain the sense that Moses would not have been the only biblical author or character that could join the D6 Conference Speaker lineup. Joshua, Hezekiah, John the Baptist, and Paul all influenced parents to disciple their children. Also helpful are relationships in Scripture that point the reader to good and bad examples of character traits and flaws being passed down from grandfather to father to son. The commands and principles covered are illustrated well in three generation families such as Abraham, Isaac, and Jacob. In the New Testament, Paul reminds Timothy that the influence of his grandmother and mother had a great impact on him.

While the direction was pointed out early, the destination is made plain when Hunter drives home the end goal of raising children who have a Biblical Worldview. The goal is for the next generation to carry with them an unconscious intellect or a second nature response in making decisions, handling emotions, and thinking on issues. Hunter makes the analogy of a battleship that is built for war by being equipped not for defense but for a posture of offense. He argues that the best defense for parents is a strong offense, so the goal should be to "launch" kids out ready to do battle in the fields of apologetics, ethics, and theology. To arrive at that destination, the author argues that parents must go beyond teaching their children the names of the biblical patriarchs and the details of the narrative to get to the concepts of Scripture and the experience of application. Families must dive through the who and the what and reach the depth of the why and how. The author does not take a shortcut or call for parents and teachers to bypass the surface facts and figures, but rather calls them to go through them and beyond. Using Bloom's Taxonomy as a guide, *The DNA of D6* shows stair steps to take in reaching the goal of teaching and discipleship.

At the end of the book, a very useful analogy is given to help parents take this dive into deeper conversations. In the setting of a vacation to the beach there are opportunities to build sand castles, do some snorkeling, or go scuba diving. Sand castles are built on the surface. This is where most people stay. Snorkeling stays near the surface and takes periodic and short plunges. Scuba Diving goes deep and stays deep to explore where very few go. To reach the goal of the Biblical Worldview, a battleship ready to be launched out, it will take some deep dives into the concepts and principles of Scripture.

True to the practical nature of the book, concrete next actions steps for churches are covered in the remainder. From the larger perspective of church organization and leadership strategy to the more specific area of types and functions for small groups, the steps are specific and helpful. Hunter points to the need for churches to rethink placing youth ministry on the outside of the larger body's strategy and methodology. Putting the youth ministry outside of the main life of the body and then expecting those students to seamlessly transition back into life in the church is short sighted and ill conceived. Not surprisingly, Hunter recommends using curriculum to align all of the ministries in one direction and all on one subject. While Hunter leads a publishing house and it's no surprise he recommends the use of curriculum that puts all ages on the same page each week, his argument is strong. Especially considering the conversations among families and most importantly between parents and children that this strategy will foster. The argument of D6 is when all groups are already on the same subject, the parents and mentors are well equipped to take the conversations deeper and live out the call of Deuteronomy 6 to talk of the things of the Lord as they walk by the way, sit down to eat, and lay down to sleep.

Ron Hunter is undaunted to cover one of the most personal reasons that some struggle with generational discipleship. Though subject matter is difficult, Hunter addresses the reason that many church leaders struggle to champion the generational discipleship, the subject of prodigal sons and daughters among their own families. *The DNA of D6* wades into the pain these leaders face. Recognizing the integrity that pushes leaders to refrain from calling their people to something they have not lived themselves, the text assures them that it is not hypocrisy to help parents achieve what the leaders dream of for their own families. In addition to covering this personal hurdle that many leaders have to overcome, the book closes with encouragement and advice to persist through the challenge that all leaders face: Changing their organization's culture. There is no glibness here. While *The DNA of D6* definitely lifts up an ideal that will be difficult to achieve, the closing words are realistic about the fact that this shift will take time. Patience, collaboration, and leadership are required to make any change and the same holds true for a church that moves to effective generational discipleship. Hunter does not call ministers to implement a new program and consider their work done. He pleads with leaders to steward their influence, cautions them against groupthink, and advises translating the concepts into the context of their church's strengths and weaknesses.

Hunter is passionate about generational discipleship and churches that are helping families disciple their kids. This passion for the discipleship a new generation of believers has produced a book to help these churches align their ministry with families. Leaders of churches of all shapes and on all points of the discipleship journey will find this short book to be a very practical guide, directing them toward the goal of launching out young adults armed with a biblical worldview and ready to change the world.

I would heartily recommend *The DNA of D6* to any parent or Church leader looking to incorporate this generational discipleship model into their church and home. The easy reading and practical nature make it a good fit for anyone needing a primer on the D6 model of family ministry. I believe D6 churches would greatly benefit from taking their leadership and ministry teams through the book together for discussion and application.

Adoptive youth ministry: Integrating emerging generations into the family of faith. By Chap Clark. Grand Rapids, MI: Baker Academics. 2016. 400 pp. $34.99. hardcover.

Review by Colleen Derr, Associate Professor of Congregational Formation and Christian Ministries, Wesley Seminary, Marion, Indiana.

In *Adoptive Youth Ministry: Integrating Emerging Generations into the Family of Faith*, Clark calls the reader to envision the church community as a family with youth playing a critical and unique role in the family. He clarifies that adoptive youth ministry is not adoption in terms of assimilating teens into this family in which they give-up their own identity, but rather adopting them into the family involves making room for them, welcoming them, and recognizing the value they bring. Clark suggests: "Guiding this strategy is the philosophy that a person needs to be 'in' Christian family-like community in order to be 'in Christ'" (19). He argues that the church is in need of this new, adoptive, approach to youth ministry due to three compelling realities: "we are 'losing' kids once they leave our ministry programs, there is a growing number of young people who have 'written off 'traditional' faith', and the drastic changes in the world the past few years must impact 'how we do ministry' and 'who we do ministry with'" (6-7).

The text is divided into four sections that address the context, the call, the practice, and the skills of adoptive youth ministry. There are 24 contributing authors, experts in the specific field they address based on research and experience. Section one, "The Context of Adoptive Youth Ministry," addresses the developmental realities of adolescents with Steven Bonner offering a new way to look at adolescent development that impacts how we relate and respond. He suggests that today's adolescents are experiencing delayed cognitive development and extended mid-adolescence both of which are directly impacted by the lack of adult relationships. His research and experience indicate that adolescents need "loving and sacrificial" relationships with adults who are "theologically grounded and prophetically positioned" (38). Marv Penner provides insights from research and personal experience on the wounded and broken adolescents in our communities and how we can welcome them into our ministries. He posits we must recognize that the adolescent's pain is real. Adolescents are in search of their identity and often circumstances and external forces forge a false and hurtful one. The church family offers a place where: "Young people who see themselves as outcasts, losers, or undesirable are invited into a community where they are welcomed and invited to participate" (50). The result is an "assurance that they belong" (50) and an opportunity to form a healthy identity in Christ through Christian family. In the fourth chapter Bradley Howell explores the expectations and opportunities for technology's role in ministry and concludes that adolescents need adults who are willing to join them in their online world, understand the online world from their point of view, and extend grace in the digital world (58). Craig Detweiler, in the first section's closing chapter, argues that "pop culture burrows into teens' hearts and minds in ways that sermons or Sunday school may never touch" (69) and suggests that connections are best made through observing what they watch and engaging in "emphatic listening" (69). Clark launches the section with a call to move away from ministry as an institution or program with defined structures, to view it rather as an organism—a family—that is adaptable. He provides the "Strategic Adoptive Ministry Funnel" as a guide for moving new participants into full members of the family (19-20). The stages of the funnel include outreach, welcoming, engaging, diverse relationships, and finally adoption.

Section two explores the "The Call of Adoptive Youth Ministry" to be reflective, ongoing, and communal. Almeda Wright contends the church community should offer youth a paradigm for faith that includes orthodoxy, orthopraxy, and critical, communal reflection (87). "Reflective youth ministry" she advises should focus on "nurturing young people to reflect the image and life of Jesus Christ and to think deeply or reflect on what it means to be a follower of Christ today" (90). A variety of authors argue that adoptive youth ministry must embrace thinking practically theologically, ecclesiologically, critically, globally, and long term. Adoptive youth ministry, Michael MacEntyre argues, must be practical theologically in that it must value humanity's story as well as God's and seek reconciliation with God and others (114). Walt Mueller continues this focus on reconciliation and community compelling the reader to gain an awareness to the current reality of youth culture, recognize that ministry to adolescents is a cross-cultural experience, contextualize ministry to the adolescent's world. The ninth chapter moves the reader beyond cultural recognition, practical theology, and reflective ministry to seeing teens as "reservoirs" rather than "receivers" (138). Mark Cannister contends that teens have something to offer now, not just something to receive and identifies specific ways we can embrace teens in making connections and contributions to the faith community. Allen Jackson offers five things teens need from the faith community: "A creed to believe in," "a community to belong to," "a call to live out," "a hope to build on," and "a world to share" (163) and concludes that the means to achieving all of these are intergenerational, authentic relationships.

The practice of adoptive youth ministry is the focus of the third section with chapter topics that include how to create a welcoming space and a culture where questions are welcome. Pamela Erwin provides three theological arguments for creating a welcoming space: "God's invitation includes 'whosoever will' into a relationship with Him and His people"{, "the reign of God extends beyond the doors of the local church," and "youth ministries are 'launching pads' not the destination" (200). She further encourages the reader to embrace a culture of Shalom—"generous hospitality" (203). Kara Powell and Brad Griffin share that the results of a longitudinal study on the faith of young adults suggest a significant number (70% in their study) of students have doubts about their faith, but less than half of those feel free to ask questions within their ministry settings to clarify those doubts (223). Safety and support are necessary ingredients in helping a teen navigate these doubts, and an adoptive community of faith is an ideal place to create safe relationships, space for questioning, and support for seeking. Spiritual formation with adolescents as well as the unique call to middle school ministry, urban, multi-ethnic, and Latin-American settings are additional topics covered in this third section. Tony Jones suggests that spiritual formation is "a matter of time," and that adolescents need spiritual experiences in order to experience spiritual formation: "Spiritual formation happens, guided by the Holy Spirit, when we attend to the needs of the adolescents in our care and when we provide ways for them to develop that they can handle" (220). Heather Flies identifies the unique impact of adoptive ministry on middle school students and provides specific practices to engage. Daniel White Hodge contends that urban and multi-ethnic contexts are the near future reality in youth ministry and compels the reader to understand and engage them.

The text concludes with five contributions related to the skills necessary for leading an adoptive youth ministry. These include the leadership qualities, communication skills, approach to teaching, strategy and structures that contribute, and the integration of youth ministry to the church. Leaders in adoptive youth ministry recognize their valuable role as a "bridge between the abandoned world of adolescence and the family of God" (287) and the need for volunteers and staff that model and embrace an adoptive ministry philosophy. Duffy Robbins identifies three key principles in adoptive communication. The communication of adoption: "respects the power of words" (293), "respects the power of context" (295), and "takes initiative" (296). The chapter on teaching in adoptive youth ministry answers the questions of who, when, where, and how with an emphasis on the work of the Holy Spirit. Steven Argue examines how adoptive youth ministry calls for us to rethink our strategies and ministry structures with a primary focus on the youth pastor's role and youth ministry's place in the community of faith. April Diaz carries this concept of reimagining strategies and structures further as she looks beyond the youth pastor's role in adoptive youth ministry to all those now involved due to the integration of youth in the broader scope of the church community.

Clark acknowledges that no single chapter details "how" to do adoptive ministry, but each chapter "offers a specific strategy and theology for connecting the young into the larger faith community" (8). Although each chapter is written by a different author/authors and the focus of the chapter is based on his/her personal field of research and experience, Clark weaves them together into a cohesive anthology that supports his proposed adoptive youth ministry model. The audience for the text is primarily youth pastors, leaders, directors, and volunteers although those in the "shoulder" ministries such as children, young adult, and family would also benefit. In addition, it would be a helpful read for lead pastors and other ministry leaders as the adoptive model would require church-wide acceptance in order to succeed. It is also a book that would serve well as a text for youth specific and general ministry courses as it offers not just a new model for youth ministry, but also a new approach to church-wide ministry and a new way to view intergenerational ministry. The critique of the text is that those not interested in pursuing the adoptive youth ministry model as defined in the introduction and opening chapter may miss significant contributions to the broader youth ministry field offered in the following chapters. Although these chapters support adoptive youth ministry, they offer insights independent of the adoptive model. While there is value in the concept of adoptive youth ministry, the contributions from the supporting chapters are broader in scope and potential impact than a single model.

Building Your Volunteer Team: A 30-Day Change Project for Youth Ministry. By Mark DeVries and Nate Stratman. Downers Grove, IL: InterVarsity Press. 2015. 155 pp. $16.00. paper.

Review by Randall Wright, Church Planter in McKinney, Texas where he pastors the Clearview Mission.

Whether a pastor or youth leader is familiar with Mark DeVries and Nate Stratman's previous writings or not; they would likely benefit from their latest work, *Building Your Volunteer Team*. A project published by Intervarsity Press and released in 2015, the book is subtitled *A 30-Day Change Project for Youth Ministry*. However, do not let the title fool you. The book reaches far beyond the realm of youth ministry. *Building Your Volunteer Team* addresses head-on one of the greatest challenges facing today's ministry leaders, developing a strong volunteer team. Both larger and smaller churches, rural and suburban ministries, churches led by a single pastor and multi-staffed congregations, face the need for more volunteers. Those engaged in church ministry rarely if ever hear the words, "we have more volunteers than we can use." Conversely, ministry conversations frequently revolve around how to "get enough workers" to make things flow more smoothly. In this book, DeVries & Stratman offer practical insights that will help with the volunteer gap.

Building Your Volunteer Team is structured around the belief that many churches need significant change when it comes to recruiting volunteers.

The authors' guiding presupposition is that we often find ourselves "stuck" in certain areas of ministry, unsure of how to facilitate necessary change. This book proposes that those serving in ministry usually have at least one thing in common, they are interested in change. However, much of the effort spent in ministry is in maintaining current systems and never changing them.

In establishing the need for change, DeVries & Stratman offer disturbing insight into common processes of volunteer recruitment. Findings based upon a recent research project revealed that less than one third of professional youth workers experience success in recruiting volunteers. Further investigation revealed that most of these did not have an effective system in place to help. Quoting Peter Drucker, the authors' suggest that 80-90 percent of actions in ministry are not changing anything, they merely maintain a ministry's current trajectory. As a result, for exponential change to occur, focus must shift from sustaining a single area of ministry to the development of new strategies. New strategies, however, can only be developed by new ways of thinking. DeVries and Stratman seek to provide in *A 30-Day Change Project* an avenue for the new ways of thinking and new strategy that is necessary for ministry change.

DeVries and Stratman approach is a simple step by step process, whereby they encourage those who are in need of volunteers to follow this plan over the course of 30 days. This process is described as a "recipe," "blueprint," "action plan," and a 30-day "boot camp" for those who need to create rapid change in their organization. While the process DeVries and Stratman outline can be described as simple, it also appears to be very thorough and spiritually focused. Thorough, in that they provides a daily action plan, steps to take each day for the duration of the Change Project. DeVries and Stratman also appeal to readers to take this journey with two other people, partners. These partners help create motivation and accountability. The approach also provides helpful insights in evaluating previous methods or ideology while simultaneously offering new ways of thinking about the recruiting process. The plan is also spiritual, in that it recognizes and reminds readers that ministries too often overly revolve around the leader. DeVries and Stratman seek to offset this by stressing a process that emphasizes a "rhythm" that will lead to focus and dependence on the powerful work of the Spirit. The priority of seeking to make this process a spiritual exercise is further supported by the role that the "partners" play. They are prayer partners that the minister is encouraged to regularly meet with and update throughout the recruiting process. Through weekly updates covering the previous week's efforts and through sharing items to pray about during the upcoming week, the prayer partners are important spiritual partners encouraging and assisting the minister seeking to implement change.

The "rhythm" that DeVries and Stratman speak of consists of breaking the 30-day plan into weekly segments that offer different tasks for each day, while also incorporating certain repetitive actions or days throughout the four weeks. Each week contains what I would classify as *prepare, work, and rest.* The week is broken down into five days of activity, tasks, and duties. Each of these days contain recruiting concepts that will help to initiate change in process. Every day concludes with a mission to accomplish for that day. These five days are sandwiched between what DeVries and Stratman call a "Balcony" day at the front of the week and a "Reflection" Day at the end of the week. While these days do not have significant tasks assigned to them, they do provide significant benefits. Balcony days are designed to provide an opportunity for the minister to gain weekly clarity along this journey. According to DeVries, this day allows one time to work not just *in* the project and ministry but rather work *on* the project or *on* their ministry; a thirty-thousand-foot view from above, as he describes it. Reflection day follows the five days of directed tasks. This day provides an opportunity for Sabbath. A day designed to rest and allow God to do His work, recognizing that we are not in control. This day also is designed to create time for thinking through your meetings and time with your prayer partners. This idea of "rhythm" aptly describes the weekly process. DeVries and Stratman make a convincing case that structuring rhythm into the process will help easily "move" an individual toward the necessary change in recruiting.

Another benefit one will find by acquiring *Building Your Volunteer Team* is the resources that DeVries and Stratman makes available through throughout the book and the related ministry website, ministryarchetects. com. Anyone who has spent time recruiting volunteers understands the additional challenges often associated with creating a quality volunteer ministry. There are the initial letters that may be sent out in the recruiting process. Then those who are responsible for building a volunteer base are inevitably going to be called upon to create and then communicate the expectations that are associated with a place of responsibility. This requires defining the roles of multiple levels of ministry involvement, and possibly being the voice to communicate the need for volunteer background checks. The amount of information to create and communicate can be overwhelming, if left to figure it out on one's own. Thankfully, DeVries and Stratman provide sample communication tools to assist in both instruction and in improving your recruiting process. There are sample email templates to previous workers and prospective volunteers. They even provide eight (8) different suggested phone conversations that you can use in a sequential and progressive attempt at recruiting an individual to serve in an area of ministry. *Building Your Volunteer Team*, is filled with helpful information and resources from beginning to end. In addition to the sample templates and communication resources that are a part of the body of the book, DeVries and Stratman offer additional resources in the Appendices of the book. Offering sample youth calendars and Surveys to review and plan for major youth events and additional areas of improvement.

Overall, DeVries and Stratman have provided an excellent resource for those who have been given the task of staffing a volunteer ministry. Although the book is a quick and easy read, it provides tremendous encouragement and thought provoking material to challenge readers stuck in the way things have always been done. Reminding readers of what really matters in volunteer ministry this book is truly a practical step by step guide that offers simple and doable tasks.

I suppose the last positive element of the book is found on the back cover—a money back guarantee! According to the authors, "If you work this 30-day process for one to two hours a day, six days a week, for 30 days and it does not create significant change in your ministry, Ministry Architects will gladly refund the cost of the book and offer a credit of $20 toward any downloadable resource in our online store." It appears that those who are in need of either some help in creating a strategy to enlist more and better volunteers or finding a new way to think about volunteer ministry have nothing to lose by purchasing *Building Your Volunteer Team*; and quite possibly may have the opportunity of obtaining both or in the worst case scenario simply enjoying $20.00 worth of free ministry resources!

What is D6?

BASED ON DEUTERONOMY 6:4-7

A **conference** for your entire **team**

A **curriculum** for every age at **church**

An **experience** for every person in your **home**

Connecting
CHURCH & HOME
These must work together!

D6 CONFERENCE
ONCE A YEAR

DEFINE & REFINE Your Discipleship Plan

www.d6family.com

ONE HOUR
A WEEK

POWER OF
PARENTAL INFLUENCE

Family Ministry Resources

How You Always Meant to Parent
by Brian Housman

Setting aside the distractions of today to focus on your legacy of tomorrow

ISBN: 9780892656745
PRICE: $14.99

Five Reasons for Spiritual Apathy in Teens
by Rob & Amy Rienow

What can parents do to help spiritual apathy in teens?

ISBN: 9780892659883
PRICE: $9.99

Practical Family Ministry
by Timothy Paul Jones and John David Trentham

A collection of practical family ministry ideas for you to implement in your church

ISBN: 9780892659876
PRICE: $13.99

The DNA of D6
by Ron Hunter

The DNA of D6 shares great strategies for all family ministries. It builds on the foundation of a timeless philosophy found in Deuteronomy 6.

ISBN: 9780892656554
PRICE: $14.99

The Legacy Path
by Brian Haynes

Discover Intentional Spiritual Parenting

ISBN: 9780892656349
PRICE: $11.99

Surviving Culture Parent Edition
by Edward E. Moody

When Character and Your World Collide

ISBN: 9780892659838
PRICE: $9.99

Building Believers through Church & Home

•• More titles available at D6FAMILY.COM ••

CPSIA information can be obtained
at www.ICGtesting.com
Printed in the USA
LVOW01s0042040316

477733LV00007B/7/P

9 780892 659852